Ellen, Discovered

Ellen, Discovered

A MEMOIR OF MY MOTHER

Karen Gooen

BUBBE MEISES PUBLISHERS

ISBN: 978-0-9907601-4-6 (paperback book)

978-0-9907601-8-4 (ebook)

Cover and book design by Duane Stapp

Printed in the United States of America

First Printing 2024

Contents

For Ellen

זיכרונה לברכה

Zichrona livracha—may her memory be a blessing

Foreword

My mother passed away on a Sunday afternoon, at home, as she had requested. Two days later, after the funeral, my daughter, Elizabeth, was looking through books and boxes on Mom's bedroom shelves.

"I hear her voice saying, 'Quit snoopin' around!'" she laughed.

We found costume jewelry, cards and letters from my dad she had saved, and emails she'd printed out from her grandkids.

Elizabeth also found a decoratively carved wooden container, about the size of a cigar box. It didn't have a normal lid. She recognized it was a puzzle and slid the panels in a certain way to open it. It appeared to be empty, but upon closer inspection she realized it had a false bottom, under which she found photographs.

Elizabeth called out to me. "Mom, come here, you have to see this!"

She handed me a few square black-and-white prints. I recognized my mother immediately, and clocked her as somewhere in her teens, but none of her companions looked familiar.

Elizabeth later told me that my immediate response was, "Oh, poor Mom."

My next statement, in my head and then aloud, was, "I know what this is about."

Chapter 1
"Mommy and Me"

My mom and I had a lot in common. Each of us was a third child. We both skipped a grade and graduated from high school at age sixteen and college at twenty. We were Sagittarians with a quick wit, heavy on the sarcasm. We each stayed home to raise our kids. We didn't focus on housework, much to our respective mothers-in-law's dismay. In later years, I liked to say that my siblings and I were "raised by wolves—very intelligent wolves."

Mom had been an elementary school teacher, and she prioritized my education, both artistic and academic. She signed me up for piano and dance lessons and indulged me by making up math worksheets, something I liked to do for fun. When I showed interest in guitar, she picked out a three-quarter-size, nylon-stringed acoustic "for the family" that somehow ended up in my bedroom. She often dropped me off at the public library—a place I loved, where I would spend hours alone in the stacks.

My older siblings' passions were encouraged as well. My brother played many different sports, but the most important were football, basketball, and baseball. The entire family attended every contest and game—including the Gino's Super Shooter and NFL Punt, Pass, and Kick competitions. I chose to spend those afternoons in the grandstands reading a book, or under them, looking for loose change. It wasn't until I noticed these events included boys other than my brother that I showed any interest in the goings-on.

My mother drove my older sister Jojo to gymnastics studios and crafting classes focused on things like making miniature accessories for dollhouses. She would often take Jojo to a local shop, Craft, Kit and Caboodle, to find a new project. Mom threw great kids' birthday parties; ours were always fun, with clever games and activities like do-it-yourself stuffed animals or Shrinky Dinks. To be honest, we looked down on the kind of parties where the main events were chasing one another, popping balloons, and watching the birthday kid open their presents.

Our family was Jewish, but my parents gave us minimal exposure to its formal institutions and liturgy. Most of our Jewish peers in suburban Maryland were affiliated with the local Conservative or Reform synagogues, attending Shabbat services, learning Hebrew, and becoming bar and bat mitzvahs. My siblings and I barely skimmed the surface of religious education at our weekly half-day Sunday School. We were taught American Jewish history, and we learned about Jewish holidays through music and food—not that there's anything wrong with that.

Purim—the holiday where the Megillah, the story of Queen Esther, is read—was done up well at our Jewish Community Center. It included a carnival with games and prizes. There were special songs and skits, as well as treats like hamantaschen, the three-sided cookies meant to resemble the Purim villain's hat (or ears, depending on the translation).

The JCC also held a Purim costume parade. One year, I opted not to dress up as Queen Esther, something almost all the girls did. Instead, I chose to go as Vashti, the proud and disobedient first wife of the King—wearing one of my mother's silky bathrobes and a scowl on my face as I carried a well-labeled suitcase. (Vashti had refused to dance naked for the king's friends; as children, we were told that Vashti was banished, but in fact, she was executed. Ancient Persia was a rough place.)

Mom loved that I chose to do that. She recognized the kind of daughter she was raising: an outspoken, independent-minded Vashti among all the pretty, agreeable Esthers.

Our home life lacked *Yiddishkeit*—European Jewish customs, including culture, cooking, and language. I picked up most of my early Yiddish terms and Jewish sensibility from *MAD Magazine* and comedians like Alan King. We were so secular, in fact, that we put up a Christmas tree and stockings by our fireplace every year. It's true that we lit the candles on the hanukkiah, but we put our presents under the tree and exchanged them on the morning of December 25. Our house had a distinct odor of pine and fresh-baked cookies. I remember trying to explain this in elementary school by saying that one of my great-grandparents was Christian. This was completely untrue, but I didn't know how else to justify the extent of our assimilation.

I knew my father's mother, Sarah, wasn't happy about this aspect of our upbringing, but I was too young to understand why. She made a point of telling us our presents were for Hanukkah, rather than Christmas, and welcomed us to Passover seders at her home in

Forest Hills, Queens. We spoke on the phone every week, but only saw her twice a year, so her influence was limited.

I recall attending the JCC's original nursery school program before they had broken ground on a physical building. They had to rent space at a Catholic church nearby. One day when Sarah was visiting, we were driving in that neighborhood, so I pointed out my preschool. My grandmother, seeing a church and little else, said, "Where is it, darling? I don't see anything."

I also remember going to the circus one April and sitting near school friends who had brought their own kosher-for-Passover snacks. It made me realize, in a very tangible way, that there was a whole world of identity and observance I was missing. I wanted to understand what it meant to be Jewish.

As soon as I found out that the Sunday School had a library, I embarked upon my own cultural education, reading as many biographies and novels about Jewish families as I could. I focused on heroines like the five sisters in the *All-of-a-Kind Family* books, and I knew whole scenes from Johanna Reiss' Holocaust memoir, *The Upstairs Room*, by heart. For years, in my head I called the bad guys I read about "Nay-zize." It took me a long time to realize that they were the same villains as the "Not-sees" that were in all the World War II movies. That's the kind of thing that happens when a person reads a lot on their own, but isn't exposed to topics in regular conversation.

We attended an open elementary school, with mixed grades and self-guided "centers," rather than traditional desks and teacher-focused learning. (It was the 1970s, after all.) My mom came in as a volunteer, helping individual students who might have missed out on fundamentals, but she also loved working with the more gifted kids, offering enrichment sessions. She took special pride in their later successes, including a certain Ivy League dean who became a university president.

My mother always made sure we had a strong secular education. By October, when my first-grade teacher got tired of me raising my hand and answering all the questions, Mom agreed to my moving up a grade—but insisted that I never be placed in the same mixed-grade classes as Jojo, who was two years older but now only one grade ahead. We had one class together in ten years, when the high school had to combine levels four and five of French.

Mom advocated for us to be assigned to the best instructors, regardless of the peer environment. I figured this out when my schedule, which was always tracked with the same group of high achievers, suddenly veered off for a particular subject. My mom had told the guidance office to move me to the class led by "the other guy," the one who wasn't making suggestive comments to young girls or showing movies rather than teaching. She attended Back-to-School Night all the way through my senior year of high school, even though both my older siblings had already had many of the same teachers. That's the kind of mother she was.

Mom and I went through a bit of a rough patch when I was in high school. I was the first kid in the family to flaunt curfews, to drink alcohol at parties (wine or beer, never the hard stuff) and come home tipsy. On the scale of adolescent behaviors, I'd like to point out that I was quite tame (no cigarettes or drugs, stayed a virgin, always made the honor roll), but she'd had two super-strait-laced kids before me. Despite the foreshadowing when I chose to be Vashti, she seemed unprepared for my minor teenage rebellion. I can't recall the specific discussion, but when I was fifteen, we were arguing and I slapped her—and she slapped me right back.

I think my mother enjoyed having me around. I was somewhat challenging, with the curfew-breaking and the backtalk, but I was never boring. I participated in all sorts of clubs and activities, so even when I was grounded for bad behavior, I still had people counting on me to be places. Copyediting the newspaper at the printer's shop and attending math, speech, and academic competitions necessitated staying out long after school hours, traveling all over the county, and *hey*—a kid's got to eat, right? Also, as the team statistician, I was required to go to all the varsity baseball practices and games. I *had* to sit outside on sunny spring afternoons with seventeen high school boys. It wasn't what anybody else's standard for grounding would have been.

I have few memories of my mom and dad during my college years. Sending three kids to college at the same time was an expensive proposition on a government salary. We moved away from my childhood home in Maryland soon after I graduated so that my father could get a better-paying job. I ended up feeling uncomfortable in "my parents' house," a half hour west of Boston. I spent as much vacation time as possible with my serial-monogamous string of boyfriends and their families.

My father wasn't a fan of my choice of academic institution. My college was as unstructured as my open elementary school had been—possibly more so. He had sent two kids to Yale, who both majored in molecular biophysics and biochemistry, the hardest pre-med major at the university; meanwhile I was, in his opinion, "futzing around," studying political science at S/NC (Satisfactory/No Credit), lowest-grade-is-a-C Brown. It was much easier to avoid coming home rather than listen to his judgments.

During a post-college year in Boston, I seemed to redeem myself in his eyes when I was accepted at Columbia University graduate school, where I would study developmental psychology. I went to live with my parents then, who had moved to Westchester County.

This was a new parallel between Mom and me. She had lived at home when she attended school in Morningside Heights and took the 1 train (or a bus) about two miles north from her West End Avenue apartment in Manhattan to Barnard, Columbia's women's college.

Thirty-three years later, I, too, lived with my parents. My dad and I drove in every weekday from Westchester to the Washington Heights medical campus. I had a part-time job in the development office of Babies Hospital, the pediatric division of Columbia Medical Center. In the afternoons, I took the elevator at the West 168th Street subway station—which felt, circa 1986, like I was heading down a mine shaft, perhaps never to see daylight again—descending into the bowels of Upper Manhattan to go two miles south to the main Columbia campus and Teachers College. After class, I would catch a Metro-North train from Grand Central Terminal back to Westchester, sometimes arriving home as late as 11 p.m.

During that year, I got to know my parents on a different level. I'd already lived independently in Boston, with a job and my own income. I expected to be home for that one year, knowing the next time I moved out would be "for good." They had to accept me as an adult.

My father and I spent our morning commute together discussing serious topics, and we reached a better understanding of, and respect for, one another. My mother recognized that our power structure, if there had ever been one, was obsolete. There were no curfews, per se—not that it mattered: for much of the time, my parents had a far more exciting social life than I did. They went to all the Giants' home games and traveled the world for Dad's job. They sometimes went out to dinner with friends, although I think my parents loved each other's company more than anyone else's. They were each other's favorite person.

My own romantic life, upon moving back in with them, was at a low point. The previous year up in Boston had ended badly. I'd been in a serious relationship with someone from a different background. Extremely different. We met in an evening class, both of us taking lower-level psychology courses to prepare for graduate school.

When I first asked him where he had gone to college, he said, "St. John's."

"St. John's in Annapolis, the small school where you study the great books?" I asked.

He shook his head. "St. John's, the Big East basketball school near Long Island?"

Again, no.

"St. John's Seminary, just past Boston College," he explained. Seminary, as in preparing for priesthood; while we were dating, my father referred to him as "Saint Ignatius."

After much drama, our relationship did not work out, and I was miserable. My mother—out of the blue, and only once—said she, too, had been involved with someone who wasn't Jewish, and that these things often aren't meant to be. She didn't elaborate. My father's attempt at consolation was, "Well, now you're ready to settle down"—implying, of course, that it would be with a Nice Jewish Boy.

A couple of years later, that's exactly what happened.

Chapter 2
Everything Is Fine Until It's Not

The first time I noticed my mom's cognitive decline was in the spring of 2017. She'd been living alone since my father died in October of 2000. She had chosen to stay in her large home, a quick drive from my house in suburban New Jersey.

Over the years, she might tell me about something—upcoming plans, a medical result, an issue with a contractor—more than once. I chalked that up to the fact that she had four kids (later, only three, after Jojo passed away). Maybe it was hard for Mom to keep track of what she'd said, and to whom; to be honest, if she wanted to tell a story again because she had not been able to tell my sister, I was happy to listen twice.

My mother looked younger than her age: she still colored her hair and maintained an interest in current events and culture. She traveled on senior group tours—cleverly called "Road Scholars"—and often took the train to Manhattan to go to the theater or museums or to see cousins and friends from high school and college. She went to the public library to read the weekday *New York Times*; she treated herself on the weekends by picking up the Sunday edition to read, in its entirety, at home. She swam a mile, three times a week, at the indoor pool of a local hotel. That was another favorite topic of hers, but only when things went wrong: "The heater is broken so they wouldn't let me swim today… They're redoing the locker room, so it's closed for a week… They're having a preschool swim class—I don't think I want to go on Tuesday mornings anymore."

Mom also traveled to the weddings of each of her five Israeli-American grandchildren. She'd had what appeared to be heart issues at age seventy-one, while attending my oldest nephew's wedding, and my brother the cardiologist told her to see a doctor when she returned to the States. It turned out she needed emergency surgery to implant a pacemaker. I was on a cruise in the Pacific Ocean at the time for Thanksgiving break. I heard the whole story after the fact, when she was recovering. It was an example of her fierce independence, not wanting to complain or ask for help.

Even before she got the pacemaker, Mom had a disturbing history of ignoring health issues. One epic example of her stubborn self-sufficiency was in 1998 at my parents' summer house in the Berkshires. Mom had developed an allergy to bee stings over several years; although they hadn't been a problem in her youth, she'd experienced some itching and hives after the last one and her doctor warned her that she might need medical attention "next time it happens."

When Mom got stung again, she was alone in the backyard. She remembered her doctor's words and decided she should get to an emergency room. Not via ambulance—it was just twenty minutes away, she could drive herself!

This took place during a period of major controversy in the area about one of the main roads that ran alongside a lake for about a mile. There was ongoing debate even after a concrete barricade had been installed between the road and the lake. "Pro-wall" advocates talked about improved safety, while "anti-wall" folks said it was obstructing the view.

My mother was about five minutes from the hospital, along that specific stretch, when she passed out behind the wheel. The barricade stopped her car from plunging into the lake. When the EMT crew got to her, she was revived enough to mumble, "Bee...sting," before losing consciousness again.

For a moment, she was a celebrity. The local newspaper's editorial cartoonist had a field day with it: he ran a panel strip about how bee "thugs" had been hired to stir up more trouble in the wall debate. He sent Mom the original, signed artwork.

She continued to disregard her own health issues. In 2000, as my father was dying of pancreatic cancer, she started having symptoms of what turned out to be endometrial cancer. She said and did nothing about it; she wanted to spend as much time as possible by Dad's side at the hospital. She was not willing to go see a GYN-oncologist until after he passed away.

Jojo was a hematologist/oncologist. She stayed with Mom, attentive as Mom had been to my dad, making sure Mom got through her surgery and treatments without a hitch. When Jojo passed away three years later, I made a point of telling everyone she'd saved Mom's life.

Ever since her youth, Mom had loved Broadway theater. She kept *Playbills*, the official programs, from every show she'd seen, whether good or bad. She loved to tell stories, like the time she went to see *The Pajama Game*: the star, Carol Haney, was out sick and her understudy took over—a young lady named Shirley MacLaine.

More recently, Mom found a special place in her heart for Lin-Manuel Miranda. Like the people at the MacArthur Foundation, she thought he was a genius. She took my son to see *In the Heights* on Broadway and said her favorite part was watching *him* watch the opening scene.

Mom was the first person in the family to know about *Hamilton*, which she saw when it was still at The Public Theater. Elizabeth remembers going to Barnes & Noble with her, circa mid-2015, when my mother berated a media department clerk. That poor kid told her the store didn't have the *Hamilton* cast recording; worse still, he didn't seem to know anything about the show. Mom bought the CD as soon as it became available, and I made sure to get tickets for her and my son when it headed to Broadway.

At age eighty, things began to change for my mother. She fell victim to the "grandson scam," where someone calls up and says, "Hi, Grandma, it's me." He never gives his actual name, and if asked, says, "Don't be silly, Grandma, you know it's me! Don't you recognize my voice?" The grandparent is slightly embarrassed at this and says, "Of course I know you, sweetheart!"

The putative grandson begins to tell an alarming tale of being in trouble and in desperate need of money. The grandparent is let in on his confidences: "Don't tell Mom and Dad, I don't want to upset them or make them mad. It'll just be between you and me, I really need your help." Just our little secret, etc. Not only is her dear grandchild in peril, but he is coming to her above his own parents; she is flattered, and a little excited to still be a part of the action.

This specific caller told my mom that he needed cash quickly in order to get out of a terrible situation: he was alone, in a jail cell, in a foreign country. Mom drove to local convenience stores and wired amounts just under $1,000 several times, to various addresses overseas, yet the caller continued to need her help. He explained that complications had arisen. Beyond bail, there were medical costs, legal fees, and people to pay off at the embassy. The scam could have gone on for days if she hadn't called me, all excited, to tell me that she was going to pick up my oldest nephew at Newark Airport.

The scammer had told some very elaborate lies. The story was set up such that he had gotten into a car accident after getting drunk at a wedding in the Dominican Republic. It did not seem like plausible behavior from my nephew, a relative teetotaler and father of four kids. Based on Mom's responses, he embellished the airport part as a promise to stop and see her "on his way back home." Although he never said so, my mother assumed he meant Israel, yet the plans involved traveling late on a Friday afternoon—something my nephew would never do lest he be stranded or still in transit during Shabbat.

None of this made sense. I called my brother in the middle of the night, Israeli time, to verify that in fact his son was at home, three blocks away from him, and had not traveled to the Dominican Republic. Half-awake and confused, my brother confirmed my suspicion. I rushed over to my mother's house, and the first thing I did was hug her. It was an introduction to how fragile she was becoming and gave me a small taste of what lay ahead.

I stuck around her house past 10 p.m., waiting for an opportunity to confront the person who'd defrauded my mother. Lo and behold, the phone rang. I grabbed it before she could pick up.

"Hi, Grandma, it's me. I need more help."

"What's your name, honey?" I asked.

"Oh, come on, Grandma, stop playing. You know it's me!"

I slowly and deliberately repeated, "What's…your…name?"

He hung up, never to be heard from again.

After that, I started noticing things.

Mom had always been on top of her finances and health information, her schedule, the news, but now began to ask questions about things that used to be second nature. I only found out about the "grandson" scam when she called to ask me how to get to Newark Airport, something she had done at least fifty times over the years.

She still seemed capable of doing her own shopping and banking, and drove herself to her numerous doctors' appointments, but I decided I should accompany her for her trip to her fifth Israeli grandchild's wedding in the fall of 2018. We traveled together without any problems, but I wondered how she would have navigated if I had not been with her.

More time passed. In May of 2019, we planned a trip to her great-nephew's high school graduation party in the Maryland suburbs. I'd drive her down and drop her at my younger sister's house in DC for two nights, then we would all meet up at the party. Afterward, I would drive her and Elizabeth back to New Jersey.

Mom must have called me four or five times to reconfirm the schedule. My sister called me to tell me that Mom had been calling her, too, several times a day, asking where she was supposed to be and when. It wasn't like Mom to be so confused about plans.

The trip, after all her worrying, went off without a hitch. Mom got to spend time with her brother and a beloved cousin, and I was happy that all three generations could be together.

Back in New Jersey, she called me a few days later, sounding very worried. She told me she'd given her social security number over the phone to someone who had offered to help her fix her computer. Another scam! I told her we'd go to the Social Security office on Monday morning, and we would need to bring some documents with us.

That was the tipping point. She called me every five minutes, worrying about whether she could find all of the documents and where she should put them. I told her that my husband, Michael, and I would take her out to dinner that evening, and afterward we would come inside and help her find everything. We did, and I put the documents in a Ziploc bag with a sticker on it that said, "for Monday," thinking I could get a moment's rest. She continued to call, anxious about what she had done and what "for Monday" meant.

Our visit to the Social Security office was unproductive. They had heard similar stories before. They recommended she get LifeLock to protect her identity and suggested we monitor her credit report.

We stopped at Staples and I bought her some phones with built-in caller ID. I tried to explain that she should not answer calls from anyone except her doctors, her friends, or me and my siblings…but that was like trying to put your finger in the dike as the flood waters surged.

I called LifeLock and found she already had an account with them. On the one hand, it was frustrating to learn she wasn't aware of existing relationships, but it was a relief to know her credit was already being monitored. I put a formal block on any new loans or credit cards being requested in her name.

Strange things continued to happen. She couldn't find her checkbook, so she ordered more checks—several times. Despite the caller ID, she answered phone calls from strangers. She gave out her utility account number to various cold callers so that her electricity supplier switched multiple times in the course of six months. At the time, each of these things made me apoplectic: "Stop answering strangers' calls!" "Stop giving out personal information!" "Go look in the closet, there are two hundred blank checks in there!"

I tried to get a handle on things. That summer, I accompanied her to every medical appointment so I could develop a relationship with each of her doctors. I would need to know everything about her medical situation. I also got her to recognize it was time to set me up with durable power of attorney, with the expectation that I would soon need to step in and assume her financial responsibilities. As with the doctors, I made appointments with her accountant and her financial advisor while Mom was still mostly sentient. They had encountered similar situations before, and helped me become familiar with her finances.

Another frustrating yet telling moment in that transition was when I tried to arrange for her to get a baseline brain scan. I figured that a professional might be able to see if there was any noticeable physical deterioration, over time. I asked her if she already had a neurologist and she said "no," so I asked her primary care physician for a referral.

I contacted the neurologist's office and explained I needed to set up an appointment for a new patient. When I gave the receptionist Mom's name and date of birth, I was told she had been coming to their practice for years. "She sees Dr. K. Her last visit was in February." This was even more concerning than the Life-Lock situation. It was late June, four months since she had last seen him, yet she had no recollection of the appointment or their long-standing relationship.

Granted, there were a lot of doctors to keep track of, and she'd been seeing Dr. K for her essential tremor, not anything cognitive, but it was part of a glaring trend pointing to her need for assistance. I often found her medicine all mixed up, with pills scattered on the floor or kitchen counter when they should have been consumed. It was yet another indication that she was no longer capable of independent self-care.

At the neurology appointment, where she suddenly remembered the doctor, I spoke to him about assessing her cognitive ability. He asked her some basic questions, then told me, "She's as on the ball as I am." This gave me no confidence in him or his diagnostic skills. He might have been a good neurologist for tremors, but he seemed to have no familiarity whatsoever with dementia. It is well-documented that dementia patients often "showtime" for their doctors—able to put on a strong performance for a few minutes—yet they soon recede to confusion when alone with their usual companions.

I asked him whether he could provide me with a referral to get her driving ability evaluated, hoping that an objective third party would make the decision to intervene. Her cardiologist had recommended it, sharing terrible stories of seniors who drove after they were no longer capable. He knew of accidents, including fatal ones, and "Silver Alert" situations where a confused driver was lost for hours.

The neurologist demurred but I kept pushing, and he finally gave me a phone number for the Kessler Institute, a well-regarded group in West Orange, New Jersey. Their waitlist for the assessment was six months out. I did as much driving as possible for her in the interim, rather than take any risks. We were fortunate when some snowbirds canceled; the agency had a spot available at the end of December 2019, right after my mother's eighty-third birthday.

On the way to Kessler, I didn't explain to Mom what we would be doing, but I'm not sure it would have made a difference. The evaluation had two separate components. During the first part of the exam, a technician spent ninety minutes checking her physical reaction time to light and sound, as well as her ability to follow instructions. She had a minimally adequate score, just above passing, meaning that she was eligible to move on to the second part: the road test.

I was not allowed to observe that part of the exam. The institute has its own cars, similar to driving instructors' cars, with brakes for both the driver and front passenger seats. My mom and the assessor were gone for about an hour. When they returned, the specialist said, "I just have to write up this report, it will take a half an hour or so."

Mom sat down with me and said, "Boy, she was mean! She kept on telling me I was doing things wrong. I didn't like her."

Her reactions struck me as uncharacteristically candid and immature. We sat and chatted about other things while we waited. Several times, she looked around the waiting room and asked me what we were doing there. I reminded her that she had just taken a driving test.

The evaluator called us into a private office and asked my mother a few questions. "Do you remember the truck, Ellen?"

My mother shook her head, and the woman recounted how Mom had been driving on a two-lane road and became frustrated with the slow progress of the car ahead of her. She crossed the double line, attempting to pass it, not realizing there was a truck approaching from the opposite direction. The inspector took control and was able to swerve the car back to the right before an accident occurred.

The assessor also remarked that my mother kept her eye on the speedometer a lot more than on the road.

"I wasn't used to this car, and I didn't want to speed," my mother said.

She seemed to think this was an actual DMV assessment.

"Do you remember the parking lot, Ellen?" the woman asked, and again, my mother shook her head. The reviewer explained that they did part of the assessment in a grocery store parking lot that had several internal stop signs, and my mother had ignored all of them.

I could understand that the parking lot, the testing car, and the roads were all unfamiliar to Mom. Though she only wanted to be able to drive herself for her usual errands, it wasn't worth the risk of her getting lost due to a detour, or forgetting where she was headed. Ignoring an oncoming truck was more than just a hypothetical event or a heavy-handed metaphor. I was grateful for the examiner's professional assessment that it was time to take away her driving privileges. We didn't talk about it on the way home.

When we got to her house, I preceded her into her kitchen, found the extra set of keys, and put them in my pocket. When Mom joined me, I asked her, point blank, for the keys that were in her purse. I explained that the assessment showed that she should not be driving anymore, that she was a risk to herself and others. She didn't seem happy with this, but as she handed the keys to me, the wheels in her head were still able to turn enough to remember the spares.

She jumped up to check the little box where the other set was kept, and found it empty. "Where are they?" she asked. "Where are the spare keys?"

"I'm sorry, Mom, I have to take them. You can't be driving anymore."

She became enraged. "Give me my keys. I need to drive. It's my life!" It was like talking to a teenager.

"I'm sorry, Mom. You can't have them."

She became violent. She grabbed my arm, and started shaking me. "I need the keys!"

I flashed back to the "slap" incident, which had had a quick and mutual resolution. Even forty years later, she could still summon up strength. I imagined what would happen if I gave in, if I handed the keys back to her. I knew that we would have the same fight a week, a month, maybe six months later—and in the interim she could get lost, get hurt, or hurt someone else. It was not worth taking the risk.

"I'm sorry, Mom, I can't. It's time."

She spat out some expletives I can't remember now, but she was pissed. She howled, she yelled, she said I had no right. I just stood my ground. I had no choice. I took the keys with me and left. I'm not sure how often she went into the garage to sit in that unlocked car over the next day or two, reliving memories. I hoped she would cool off.

When I returned to her house, I brought along some information from a few local charities. I said, "Where would you like to donate the car? It's in good shape."

She looked over the materials and chose The Seeing Eye. They train guide dogs for the blind or physically challenged, and she'd seen volunteers practicing with the dogs on the streets and side-walks in town. She was proud of the organization.

"I think that's a great choice," I said.

After we submitted the documentation and the donation team towed the car away, Mom was sad more than angry. The Seeing Eye people reached out to her with thanks and said they would love for her to name a dog in honor of her donation. She picked Trixie, the name of our childhood Beagle, for a hypoallergenic Boxer with a gentle and nurturing personality. Trixie has already given birth to several litters of Seeing Eye trainees.

Mom was still grousing about losing her car for the next year or so. She knew I would drive her anywhere she had to go, anytime she needed it, but I often had to explain how it had been time for her to give up the car. She recognized, as she fought me, that it meant a loss of autonomy. She had not focused at all on what it might mean for anyone's safety, including her own.

I had to be the responsible adult. The nature of our respective roles continued its reversal.

Michael and I had been planning a trip to Israel for April of 2020 and didn't want to leave Mom without supervision, so I hired a daytime companion for her, beginning in the first week of March, just before the COVID lockdown began. It was a difficult time for many people whose parents were in assisted living or memory care. Some took their aging family members out of their residential facilities, moving them back home; there was subsequently a shortage of qualified home health aides. Others decided their loved ones should remain in the facilities, while they waited and prayed, helpless, unable to visit or sometimes even communicate.

Communal living was never going to be an option for Mom. She and Dad had put Grandma Sarah in an assisted-living facility near Kessler, where she stayed until the end of her life. Every time I visited, I found it to be more than satisfactory, with activities and comfortable common rooms as well as Sarah's cozy apartment space. Mom felt differently. She told me on several occasions, "I don't want to be in a place like that. Promise me."

I began taking steps to make sure Mom could always live in her home. I had experts come in to put safety bars in the bathrooms, raise the toilet seats, permanently affix the rugs. Over the years, I had a back-up electric generator installed, as well as a ramp for the front steps and wall bars from her bed to the bathroom. I had the gas lines to her fireplaces and her stovetop disconnected because she sometimes liked to play with the jets. I had a locksmith put a second, higher lock on her front door so she couldn't wander outside; I had him back, two months later, to put locks on the basement doors because she would occasionally go downstairs late at night. Numerous appliances, including the washer, dryer, dishwasher, and oven, needed to be replaced; the air conditioner, furnace, freezer, and refrigerator needed to be serviced. Then there were the exterminators, the landscapers, the gutter cleaners, the utility companies, the cleaning crew. Caring for the house was a full-time job in itself.

It was terrible that her decline began simultaneously with the COVID outbreak. She stopped interacting with the outside world, which only accelerated her deterioration. The learning curve of adapting to an assisted-living facility would also have been hard—and I couldn't break my promise.

In a different, pre-COVID world, I might have encouraged her to try adult day programs or take her on all sorts of outings. There were any number of activities that would have kept her involved with normal life. This was not to be. Her world became tiny. I stopped taking her to doctors' offices if appointments could be done remotely. The one event for which I was willing to take her out of the house during the height of COVID was to get her allergy shots. Every month, I had to explain why she was putting on a mask, and every month she was shocked to hear that there was a pandemic.

The allergist's office staff was kind; the nurses had known her for over twenty years, ever since the incident with the crash by the lake. They, too, had witnessed Mom's deterioration—at first, she was chatty and upbeat, but over time she became more confused and had trouble navigating the building's front steps. As my mother grew worse, the nurses came out to our car, rain or shine, to give her the shots.

I began to see the monthly visits as mileposts for me to measure her orientation to the world. When I first became her chauffeur, Mom would make small talk about the places we passed:

the shops, the train station, the seasonal decorations. Over time, she became unable to recognize or process what she saw. "Boy, I haven't been down here in years," she'd say, or "I don't remember it looking like this."

Eventually she started saying things like, "It's a good thing you're driving, I have no idea where we're going." I didn't feel any pleasure in being vindicated; it was sad to see her so weak and defeated.

Whenever we were in the car, I tried tuning to Mom-friendly channels on SiriusXM. I gravitated toward the Broadway music and Sinatra stations. I recall a moment when "Satisfied," one of my favorite songs from *Hamilton*, came on. Renée Elise Goldsberry—who had won a Tony for playing Angelica, Hamilton's sister-in-law—was just starting the rap part when my mother said, "What is this? This is awful."

"It's from *Hamilton*."

She looked at me, blankly. She had no idea what I was talking about. She must have listened to that soundtrack twenty or thirty times, only a few years ago. I'd been told that music was one of the last things to leave a person's memory, but that seemed to apply only to music from her youth. I decided to limit playing the Broadway station and stuck to Big Band and Sinatra.

Possibly the most painful moment for me occurred when we were looking at a gift Mom received from the grandchildren: a frame with software that allowed you to email pictures and text to a hard drive, so that a slideshow with captions would scroll by in an unending loop. The whole family had contributed, sharing highlights from the great-grandchildren's birthday parties in Israel and snapshots of visits with the grandkids in DC. I'd even added a few events from the 1990s, including a Thanksgiving shot of me with my older sister. The text in the corner said, "Karen and Jojo, 1995."

My mother read the caption aloud and said, "Hmm. Jojo. What's she up to these days?"

My heart broke. On the one hand, it was good that she didn't remember the pain of losing a child, right? I had read about dementia patients exhibiting this kind of behavior, forgetting about events and confusing timelines. The consensus was that one should "go along with it" and not correct them. What would be the point of making her experience the trauma again?

"She's good. She's keeping busy," I said. Mom nodded and went back to gazing at the screen.

As soon as I got in my car, I called my brother to share my grief. It was one of those times when watching Mom's decline was too difficult to handle by myself.

Chapter 3
Ellen's Childhood

I want to go back, now, to share all of Mom's history, not just the years that I knew her.

My mother, Ellen Marie, was the youngest child and only daughter of parents who were middle-aged by the time she came along. She had few if any memories of her grandparents. She was a New York City girl growing up on West End Avenue, the same street as Herman Wouk's Jewish heroine, Marjorie Morningstar. Her older female cousins—already teenagers when she arrived—served as fun and fascinating role models, but she was in a generation of her own.

Mom's brothers were six and twelve years old when she was born. Her oldest brother left home when she was still very young. He served in Europe during World War II, specializing in army logistics. She knew her middle brother far better, as he remained at home until she was eleven. She adored him. He served as a military secretary during the Korean War and attended Harvard for both college and law school.

Her family was comfortable, although not wealthy, per se. One of her older cousins had married a successful and generous man, and my mother often got to experience the wider world through them. Mom liked to reminisce about the amazing view from that cousin's apartment, overlooking the Macy's Thanksgiving Day Parade route. Local family members were invited over to watch, and after the parade ended, the hostess would pass out chocolate Thanksgiving turkeys, saying that Santa Claus had dropped them off.

It was just one example of how assimilated my mother's family was. My maternal grandmother was born Esther Strulowitz, of Waterbury, Connecticut. She and her siblings were eager to rid themselves of the stigma of their Polish-Jewish roots. As adults, her brothers both changed their last name to Stanton. My grandmother did even more. Now a New Yorker, she married Jeffrey Kalt, a German Jew with American roots that predated the Civil War; one of his ancestors had been a soldier in the Union army. Eager to distance herself from the recently arrived Eastern European Jews, the young bride restyled herself as Estelle Kalt and never looked back.

Like other German Jewish American families, the Kalts had affiliated with the Reform movement. There were no Hebrew lessons, and neither of Estelle's sons had become a bar mitzvah. They had a Christmas tree in their home. Estelle, an excellent cook, made ham. My mother attended Confirmation classes at a nearby temple, but Estelle steered her away from being "too Jewish."

Estelle was, without question, the most influential person during Mom's childhood. It's hard for someone in a younger generation now to understand what it must have been like for women like her.

Before Estelle became a mother, she was a working woman—a secretary to Edward Bernays, the man who created the field of public relations. It was no doubt an interesting and challenging position for a woman who had only a high school education.

If she'd been born twenty years later, and part of a wealthier family, Estelle might have gone to college. If she'd been born forty years later, she might have been a first-wave feminist, with a career outside the home. As it was, she was a wife and mother who did not seem to relish the role. Some of my cousins have admitted to being afraid of her. In fact, the person who spent the most time up close and personal with her, my mom, had good reason to be fearful.

I have sometimes wondered whether Mom was intended. The Great Depression hit right after the birth of Estelle's second son. Estelle had grown up with brothers, and my mom was her first and only daughter. Estelle was nearly thirty-seven when Mom was born several weeks early, a preemie who required special care. Mom was known in her childhood for being petite and somewhat frail. It's hard to discern, other than dressing the child in cute outfits, what Estelle got out of the relationship.

I heard stories that made it clear Estelle had not been a warm and fuzzy Girl Mom. She was hypercritical of my mother from childhood through adulthood, and I witnessed some of it firsthand. She displayed a fondness for my brother, but would remark, to our faces, that my sisters and I should be watching our weight, or criticize how we dressed. I heard her saying worse things about us to my mother when she thought we were out of earshot.

There were certain episodes during my mother's dementia where I was convinced her anger and short-tempered responses were a replay of her childhood. She stubbornly resisted taking medications, fought against wearing certain clothing, resented being told what to do. Years before her complete physical decline, Mom had lived in fear of having "bathroom accidents"—Mr. Bernays's cousin, Sigmund Freud, would have ascribed her obsession to dramatic and punitive years of toilet training.

During my own childhood, Mom liked to recount what she referred to as "the one time Estelle did a kind thing." My mother was fascinated by pandas, and her stuffed panda was her absolute favorite toy. When Mom got scarlet fever, around age five, the doctor made a house call and told Estelle that the family had to undergo complete quarantine. Not only people, but objects, had to be removed from the home, and he insisted that all of little Ellen's toys be bagged up and sent down to the basement to be incinerated.

Despite doctor's orders, Estelle decided to rescue that panda from the bag of toys that were sitting on the back stairwell. She handed the bear back to little Ellen. Mom remembered this gesture not just because it was compassionate, but because it was an incredibly rare event—a singular maternal deed in a lifetime of criticism and disdain. Estelle's treatment of her daughter involved caviling, not kvelling.

Since she herself had not had a privileged childhood, Estelle shaped Mom's upbringing by copying the standards set by the older, wealthier cousins. Estelle and Jeff somehow found the money to send Mom away to an all-girls' summer camp in the Adirondacks and, later, an Arizona dude ranch. My mother became expert at swimming and canoeing, and a pretty decent horseback rider as well. These were the summers of polio outbreaks; perhaps that was also a motivation: to get their child, who had been born in questionable health, out of New York City and away from risk of contagion.

Another activity my mother mastered was bike-riding, something she learned in a most interesting way. A classmate, Frances

Young, lived two floors above the Kalts. Frances had received a bicycle for her ninth birthday, and she and Mom would take turns pedaling down the hallway of the Youngs' apartment, pushing off from either wall if they got too close.

Mom attended an all-girls' public high school. She was intelligent, but the academic program itself wasn't challenging. The most meaningful part for her was the friendships she made. When she graduated, her mother insisted she live at home while attending Barnard. As a commuter student, she would still be very much under Estelle's thumb.

Chapter 4

Best Friends

In June of 1955, both my parents were rising college juniors who had been hired to work in the wilderness thirty miles north of New York City. They would be residential counselors at a Fresh Air Fund camp, publicized and promoted by the *New York Times*. It was part of a charitable program that helped less-fortunate children get away from the heat and stress of an urban summer.

My grandfather, Jeff, accompanied my mother downtown to City Hall Park on orientation day. Staff would gather there to board the bus up to the camp. Mom went inside the main building to use a restroom. When she came out, Jeff was standing on the steps, chatting with a young man named Bob. Jeff introduced them.

My mother was mortified. She didn't need her father setting her up with strangers. She already wore the fraternity pin of a rising senior at Columbia. Being "pinned" was a public mark of commitment or going steady. She wasn't looking for a boyfriend.

Despite a disdainful first meeting (on her part, at least), my parents were among a group of staffers who went out to a local bar that evening. My mom said she ended up talking to my dad because he was the only other person who didn't like beer, but that didn't seem like sufficient fodder for a relationship. It's possible they had a shared sense of humor. Dad, a Cornell pre-med, was a little goofy looking, with ears that stuck out too much. On the other hand, he was charming, the president of his fraternity.

He was also a lifelong camper. His mother, Sarah, had sent him to a sleepaway camp in the Berkshires when he was four years old. Yes, sleepaway camp for a four-year-old. I can't fully express my horror that my grandmother could do such a thing. His seven-year-old brother was with him, and it was during a time when people were trying to put their children in a healthy environment, away from the City. But he was a baby!

His childhood camp was loosely affiliated with the Ethical Culture movement, guided by the same principles as Horace Mann and Riverdale prep schools in the Bronx. Although the vast majority of attendees were of Jewish heritage, the programming itself was not religious. The focus was on healthy, fun activities that instilled values like teamwork and dedication, without any formal discussion of deity. There was no obligatory prayer or kosher restriction. The biggest communal rituals were the morning sings and evening campfires.

Dad had returned there every summer since, through age seventeen, first as a camper and then as a waiter. This summer was his first in a new place. He was comfortable in the camp environment. He loved sports and games, the silly songs, and the spirit of camaraderie. On the other hand, he avoided the lakefront activities, especially swimming. All his life, he complained that the water was "too wet."

Despite his goofy looks, he was a fun guy and I'm sure that helped my mom find him appealing. They became inseparable. Uncle Selig, Sarah's brother, liked to tell us the story of how he came up to the mountains one weekend and stopped by the camp for a visit. Selig asked "where Bobby was" and was told, "He's with his best friend."

That turned out to be my mom.

Before the summer was over, the Columbia senior was long forgotten, and my mother was writing enthusiastic letters to her Barnard friends, Sally and Carol, about how she'd fallen for this guy.
There was a real advantage to being away from the watchful eye
of Estelle. Mom was able to spend time with him on a daily—and
nightly—basis, while observing how well he handled kids and responsibility. She liked what she saw.

One day that summer, in front of the entire camp community,
my father proposed. In fact, he yelled it from across the dining hall.
My mother laughed it off, but he was serious. Among her mementos was a piece of birch bark upon which he had written, "Will you
marry me?" In addition, on regular paper, he also wrote that, being
of sound mind and body, he was hereby proposing to her and would
do so every three years until she said yes.

Honestly, what's a girl to do with a rush like that?

They returned to normal life after the summer, she back to her
family in Manhattan and he to Ithaca. They exchanged frequent
letters, sometimes several times a day. His were sent to her apartment, although it is surprising that Estelle would allow such a thing.
Jeff was the one who introduced them, and I think he must have
vouched for my dad's qualities. My mom was only allowed to go up
to Ithaca with strict chaperoning.

Estelle was not fond of my father. She had high expectations
for her daughter's suitors. Despite being at the top of his class, Dad
did not have the proper background for Estelle's exacting standards.
For example, he wasn't from Manhattan and he was enrolled in the
public, state-subsidized part of Cornell, rather than a private college
like Harvard or Columbia.

She often eavesdropped on their conversations. She walked
into the living room every ten minutes or so to break up whatever
momentum they might have had going. When he visited, Estelle

expected my father to stand up each time she came in, as etiquette demanded.

Mom knew that Estelle would find fault with my dad wherever she could. After they had known one another for a week or two, Mom learned that, even though they were both set to graduate college in 1957, Dad was younger than she was by about five months. This meant that, while she was smart enough to skip a grade, he was actually even smarter, having skipped two.

Most people would be impressed by this. Mom knew that Estelle would perversely find a way to turn it into a negative. She would point out his youth and possible immaturity, and would consider it a reason to demand that they break up. I later found out that my parents never told her the truth about his age. They said Dad was born a year earlier. His birthday cakes, when in Estelle's presence, always had an extra candle to keep up the charade.

I don't know when they officially got engaged; there was a small Phi Alpha pin, then a bigger Phi Alpha pin with a diamond chip, and ultimately the ring. It was clear early on that they were going to get married, and Mom was thrilled. She loved him but was also excited about being the first girl in her class to be engaged. Had she had a more interesting career path or positive home environment, she might not have been in such a hurry. Then again, youthful hormones are pretty powerful.

She continued at Barnard for her junior and senior years and completed her degree in psychology. She found a teaching position at her own childhood elementary school and still lived in Estelle's home while my father began medical school in New Haven.

The good news was that she was able to save money for their first apartment. The bad news was that they would have to wait a full year to get married. This was the first of the wedding plans dictated by Estelle. From the date to the location to the flowers, every decision came down from above. At least they agreed on the wedding gown, a gorgeous satin hand-me-down from one of her beloved cousins.

As proof of my mom's intention to be a better parent than her mother, she allowed me full say on the details of my own wedding. In hindsight, I am sad to think she never got to plan a wedding. I value the gesture all the more because I know how difficult and contentious her own childhood was, and how determined she was to break the pattern, to not exhibit the same behavior as Estelle.

After a brief honeymoon in humid Washington, DC, Mom moved up to New Haven and found a teaching job. My dad began his second year of medical school, and they scraped by on something like $4,000 a year. In order to supplement their income, my parents bought a few hamsters from a local pet store and bred them, selling the babies back to the pet store owner for twenty-five cents per rodent. Estelle was afraid of mice and other pests, and perhaps this was part of a calculated plan to keep her from visiting frequently; it was, as they say, "a feature, not a bug."

One amazing anecdote my mother shared about Estelle and their young married life had to do with the idiosyncrasies of Connecticut law—which, at the time, banned the use of contraception for married couples. (If you're interested, see *Griswold v. Connecticut* (1965).) My newlywed mother had been to a gynecologist in New York, but now that she was living in New Haven in the late 1950s, she was unable to obtain contraceptive gels or creams to use with her diaphragm. She told my grandmother that she had "a prescription" waiting at a Manhattan pharmacy, and asked Estelle to please pick it up and bring it on her next visit.

Estelle brought it to her, but was furious. She said, "What did you ask me to get you? When I went to the pharmacy, the clerk handed me the package and leered at me, saying, 'Have a good time!'"

I find it mind-boggling just how young they were when they got married; my parents grew up together and learned to navigate the world as a team. They were true partners.

In the summer of 1960, when they were wise, experienced twenty-three-year-olds, the two city kids signed on for a summer in rural Chester, Montana. My father took a three-month internship with Dick Buker, an alumnus of Yale Medical School who was the sole physician for everyone within an approximately forty-mile radius, north to the Canadian border and west to Shelby, a town with an actual hospital. Dad got experience with all sorts of medical treatment, from preventive medicine and routine checkups to minor orthopedic surgery and obstetrics. In a pinch, he also performed emergency veterinary procedures.

They needed transportation to cover such a large territory. Neither of my parents had any experience driving a car; they had lacked both the need and the opportunity to learn. They were thrown headfirst into the situation and, frankly, it showed for the rest of their lives. Dad was a bad driver, Mom even worse. She confessed to me that she had gotten her first driver's license only because they were friends with a policeman who lived on their street in New Haven. She grandfathered her status at the DMV in every state they moved to after that.

Driving through farm fields on completely flat, endless one-lane roads; eating soft-serve vanilla ice cream and the freshest corn, steaks, and hamburgers in the world; watching shockingly beautiful sunsets across the huge skies of Montana—it was an idyllic summer. My mother was in the late second and early third trimester of her first pregnancy, and my parents were deeply in love.

They returned to New Haven at the end of the summer, and my

brother was born that October. My mother had been permitted to continue teaching through the middle of her second trimester—since it was the end of the school year—but once she became a mother, she never returned to full-time, paid work.

Her role was now strictly in support of my dad. When he chose to go into public health, she backed up his decision. They had a clear distribution of responsibilities—she was "everything inside the house" (cooking, raising us, handling the finances, cleaning—although, as I've mentioned, that was not her strength). Dad took care of things "outside the house"—both at his paying job and maintaining the yard. He raised vegetables and loved landscaping; any guest to our home was immediately taken on a garden tour, no matter the time of year. He used a riding mower—his "tractor"—and was never happier than when it snowed and he could put on the plow attachment to help out around our neighborhood. It being Maryland, that occurred at most two or three times each winter.

Dad also served as a Boys' Club coach, and eventually team doctor at the high school, when my brother played football. We were all deeply involved in the sports community. Dad never scheduled a business trip for an autumn weekend, so he could be on the sidelines for every game. Mom was friends with the other team mothers and helped run the Booster Club; my sisters and I were cheerleaders (well, for Boys' Club one year, anyway). In high school, I became a statistician, something for which I was much better suited.

We had a normal, Brady Bunch-era childhood. Mom and Dad would sometimes pile all four of us kids into the station wagon and go to a drive-in movie, hoping we would fall asleep and they could stay for the more sophisticated second half of the double feature. We went on low-budget summer road trips, and on rare occasions flew down to Sarasota, Florida, to visit Dad's (childless) aunts and uncle. We also took the Auto Train down to Florida when the Magic Kingdom first opened in Orlando.

My parents were playful with one another, although in general my mother followed whatever my father had in mind. There's a particular moment that stands out for me as her flexing just a bit. One summer in the mid-1970s, our family went to Montana to visit Dr. Buker, Dad's mentor. We camped outdoors one night, cooling our provisions in a nearby creek, and Dr. Buker brought along two of his horses in a trailer. My mother convinced my dad to go riding with her.

The horses were older and reflexively stuck together. My mother started hers out with a gentle walk, but as they moved away from our tree-shaded campsite, she upped the pace. Her horse cantered and eventually—in the open field—began a full-out gallop. The second horse followed, obediently, while my father held on for dear life. It may have lasted only sixty seconds, but Mom really enjoyed her little adventure.

My father played the long game. He got his revenge the following summer when we were touring Yosemite National Park. My mother seldom had time to read, but Frederick Forsyth's latest spy thriller had just come out and she brought it with her on the trip. My father walked into the kitchen of our rented cabin one afternoon, opened the book, and read the entire last page out loud to her. As it turned out, the final page was a coda—having little to do with the climactic scene—but Dad's intention was clear.

In general, Mom did the lion's share of childcare; it took something like her being in labor or having a medical procedure for him to supervise us, but he managed. I remember Dad driving us into the District and our walking together down the 896 steps of the Washington Monument, reading all the special state plaques along the walls, to keep busy while Mom was having minor surgery. He sometimes brought us with him on rounds on weekend mornings, which served multiple purposes: we became comfortable in a clinical environment, visiting non-contagious cardiology patients; those bedridden clients got a welcome distraction; and Mom got a little time for herself. We were also rewarded with a visit to the vending machines in the hospital's basement.

My parents handled family medical problems together well. Back in the early 1960s, Dad diagnosed a problem—over the phone—about a crisis Jeff was experiencing. He shared his opinion with a friend at a New York hospital, and that insight extended Jeff's life by more than ten years. It also finally won him some respect from Estelle.

Both parents taught me about caring for the dying when George, my paternal grandfather, was stricken with colon cancer. He had no appetite, but Mom remembered how much he loved her cheesecake and made one for Dad to bring when he visited. It was probably the only thing George ate with gusto during his final week. I kept that lesson in mind when my dad was hospitalized with his own cancer; I brought him fresh-squeezed orange juice and strawberry Fribbles (extra-thick milkshakes) from Friendly's.

As we got older, my parents began traveling together for Dad's job. Within the US, they went to conferences in La Jolla, Chicago, and New Orleans. Sometimes they went farther afield, to Europe, Japan, even Australia. They always took separate flights, like the president and vice president, hedging their bets in case something happened to one of the planes. We had visions of their aircrafts colliding in mid-air, but fortunately they never did.

Dad rose up the administrative ladder until he was director of his division, and Mom threw him a surprise party to celebrate the promotion. We kids had been trained for years to "work the room," carrying hors d'oeuvres and making small talk with international medical professionals. It was an odd life—he wasn't paid well, but he had prestige and real job satisfaction. She may have shopped at Sears and Korvette's instead of Bloomingdale's, but my mom was proud of his success; they had earned it, together.

When the financial burden became too great, Dad left the government for academia and then the pharmaceutical industry. He went from job to job and city to city while Mom did all the "inside" work, buying and selling each home and smoothing the transitions for him. They became a lot more comfortable, financially, but I suspect they were never as happy as during those early years in Maryland. At least they still had each other, but they had really enjoyed the scrappy times when all of us were young, even if money was tight. Mom never challenged his choices, but I know she missed those days.

After Dad passed away, a team from his company's human resources department made a presentation for her, showing her the stock options and insurance benefits she would be receiving. She pushed the pile of documents across the table and said, "Can I trade it all back for him, now?"

Chapter 5
The Photographs

To recap: Mom had a difficult childhood with a hypercritical mother, escaped her clutches by marrying young, and had a great marriage that ended too soon when my dad passed away at age 63 in 2000. Widowhood wasn't always lonely, but after about eighteen years, she started showing progressive cognitive decline. COVID isolation didn't help, and by the time she passed away at her home in late 2023, she had lost all her short-term memory and most of her long-term memory as well.

Which leads us to that puzzle box and the contents we discovered, inside.

One of the black-and-white shots was of my mother with a boy, both casually dressed teenagers standing by a lake. She wore a plaid shirt and jeans, and he was in a college sweatshirt and khakis. A second picture had them as half of a foursome: my mother and her guy, with a second couple. The other girl was also dressed in jeans and a blouse, and I hoped she might be my mother's friend, Sally. The faces were very tiny, and frankly I didn't know what Sally had looked like in her youth, but I thought perhaps my guess would be a lucky one.

I had been in contact with Sally throughout my mom's decline. She was my mother's closest chum and confidante. They'd both grown up in Manhattan, went to that all-girls' high school, and then to Barnard, living at home and commuting uptown to Morningside Heights. Even more significantly, Mom, Sally, and another friend, Carol (also from high school and Barnard), had all married medical students from the Yale class of 1961.

My mom married Dad after his first year of medical school, and she'd introduced Carol to one of Dad's classmates. Carol, in turn, introduced Sally to a third medical student. All three young wives were in glamorous New Haven, keeping house and raising babies, while their husbands kept horrible hours on hospital rotations and internships. They were in the trenches together, forming an unbreakable bond.

Mom talked about how they might run into one another at the local market, over by the day-old bread or the shelf of dented cans with reduced prices. They were pinching pennies, trying to exist on their husbands' meager salaries. "It's a good thing we married doctors," they'd say to one another. "Living that easy life of luxury!"

After medical school, Sally and her husband moved out to California, and later divorced. She became a therapist, remarried, was widowed, and remarried again, remaining in the Bay Area. She'd maintained touch with my mother, writing and calling and getting together in New York when Sally came East to visit her family or attend Barnard reunions. I always thought of their friendship as the gold standard. My mother told me, "You know you've got a good friend when, even if you haven't seen them for a while, you can pick up a conversation as if no time has passed."

As Mom became less active and engaged, I knew it was wise for me to reach out directly to her friends, especially to Sally. I told her that Mom wasn't checking email anymore, and while I didn't know how well she'd do on the phone, I thought she might enjoy getting brief phone calls. Neither of us brought up the possibility of visiting since it was during the peak of COVID.

Sally wrote Mom birthday cards, which she kept near and happily read over and over again. Unfortunately, the phone calls didn't have quite the same impact since she would forget them soon afterward.

I contacted Sally on the afternoon Mom passed, and we exchanged emails for several days before I asked if we could talk on the phone. I wanted to hear more stories about my mother in general, but I was also curious about whether she'd be able to give me some insight into Elizabeth's discovery. Even if Sally wasn't the girl from the other couple in the photograph, she had known Mom well during that time; it was possible she might be able to tell me something about the photos.

We exchanged texts to work out logistics and finally had the chance to speak the following Sunday morning, a week after Mom died. Sally talked about happy times with Mom, how she had always treasured their friendship, and how sad she was to think that her dear friend was gone. I shared with her how the past four years had gone, even up to Mom's final moments, and Sally said that I had done exactly the right things. I found Sally's validation comforting; it was as if Mom, herself, had given me her seal of approval.

Toward the end of the conversation, I mentioned the mementos. I said, "I know this sounds strange, but we found some black-and-white photos. I have some guesses, but I was hoping you could tell me more about them. Do you mind if I send them to you?"

She was receptive, so I texted them to her after the call. She texted back immediately.

"Oh my gosh, Karen! I remember those! Let me see if my brain can remember his name, or maybe I'll ask Carol and see if she can remember."

Sally soon called back to share some stories with me about the day the photos were taken. She and her boyfriend were indeed the other couple in the foursome.

"My boyfriend was Dave and Ellen's young man was Dave's friend, named Bill. We were having dinner at Bill's family's house. His father was a minister. Well, Bill's mother was very proper and serious and before we started to eat, she looked around and said, 'Would someone like to say grace?'"

Sally explained that this was an awkward moment for the girls. Sally was gentile but had not been brought up with any formal religious affiliation or education. Mom was, of course, Jewish. Neither of them had ever been at a Christian dinner where grace was said. As far as I know, my mom had never said any *brachot* (Hebrew blessings before a meal) either. Ever.

Sally described how she and Mom looked at each other with great unease. After several beats, Mom's boyfriend broke the suspenseful silence by flippantly saying, "Grace!"

"That's the kind of guy he was," Sally said. "Sweet, silly, really down to earth."

She said she thought Mom and Bill dated for about a year, and that it was a huge deal at the time because both the young men were in college, while she and my mom were still in high school. "We thought we were such hotshots, dating college men!"

I had kept Mom's brief comment, about things not working out when she dated a non-Jew, in a special place in my memory. Now Sally was describing a boy Mom dated who came from a different religious background. With the insight that his father was a minister and his mother was somewhat stiff, in that old Yankee kind of way, it was pretty clear to me which family was more concerned about religion and had forced the breakup. After all, Estelle was so eager to assimilate that she had erased every bit of her Eastern European Jewish lineage via Christmas trees and ham.

I asked Sally, "How did a New York City high school girl come to date a minister's college-boy son in Connecticut? How would she even meet such a person?"

Sally explained that her grandparents lived up in Fairfield County, Connecticut. She often went to visit them and started dating Dave, a boy who lived nearby. Dave asked if she had a friend he could fix up with his friend Bill, who lived in a neighboring town, and that's how it began.

Mom's date was wearing a Penwell College sweatshirt in the photo. I asked if either or both of the boys had gone to Penwell. "Yes, I know Dave did. I think they both did."

She couldn't remember much else. She didn't remember exactly why they broke up but she knew that he'd meant a great deal to my mom. "He was a sweetheart," she said. "Ellen was very sad when it ended. But she was destined to meet your dad!"

It all made sense. On a separate occasion, in a conversation of no real importance, my mom had mentioned an ex-boyfriend who went on to teach high school in Connecticut. I tucked that information in the same special corner of my brain as her comment about the non-Jewish boyfriend; it had occurred to me, at the time, that both remarks might well be about the same person.

When Elizabeth showed me what was hidden away in the false bottom of that box, I suspected I was looking at "Poor Mom" with that mystery beau; after talking with Sally, I was absolutely certain.

Chapter 6
One Thousand Words or Less

U p to this point, reader, I've only told you about two black-and-white images taken with a Brownie camera: Bill, in his Penwell sweatshirt, arm in arm with blue-jean-clad Mom by a lake; and Bill, Mom, Dave, and Sally by the same lake.

I haven't described the other two prints, which were not taken with a Brownie. They were printed on different types of paper and varied in size; they were also taken indoors. One is of Bill lying on a hammock, hands crossed behind his head, staring dreamily into space.

And then there's the photo that compelled me to take on this project. As the saying goes, a picture paints a thousand words. Here are a few hundred, anyway…

My mother looks young yet sophisticated, with clear skin and a cute pixie haircut, like Audrey Hepburn in *Roman Holiday*—a film that came out at the end of summer 1953, around the time of this visit. Bill is nice looking—a clean-cut guy with a straight, non-Mediterranean nose. He also has clear skin. It's hard to tell in black-and-white, but his hair and eyes do not appear jet black the way hers do. His hair is neat and slightly wavy, not too long but not a crew cut.

Mom is sitting on his lap, her right arm around his shoulder; his left arm is around her waist. Their bodies seem almost conjoined. He is in a slightly-too-large tan blazer, a collared white shirt, and dark pants. He may be wearing a tie, but we can't see it. The picture is taken from behind Mom. She is in a daring, black, backless and sleeveless halter-top dress.

She has turned her head so that she and Bill are both looking at the camera, but it's not a posed picture. It is the definition of a candid shot. In fact, their faces are so close together—her lips millimeters away from his eyes—that it's obvious that they had been in the middle of something intimate and had not expected anyone to be watching, let alone snapping photos. Her eyebrows are slightly raised and her eyes are wide.

I've seen this look before, on my kids, and I'm sure I've made the same face several times myself. She showed surprise, even a little shock, that she had been discovered. And yet their bodies are so intertwined, so clearly "owning" one another, that there's also a certain defiance and power in her face. The photographer found Mom in a moment when she was exactly where she wanted to be.

Bill's eyebrows are also raised in surprise, but he seems bemused, calm, and comfortable. Based on their semi-formal outfits and the streamers coming down from the ceiling, they appear to be at a party. They could be in a basement or a social hall, it isn't clear. He's sitting on a plain, wooden, armless chair, and there's a low bookshelf next to him. What at first look like dueling swords on the wall turn out to be traditional, New England Puritan-style candleholder sconces.

The look on Mom's face screams, "I'm not in Estelle's living room anymore." I loved the image immediately. I needed to know more about the girl who is captured in this shot, the girl who is capable of this moment. I'd never met her, and I had certainly never seen him. I wanted to know the rest of the details.

This is a great story, I need to write a book about it. That's how I process things. I need to think about them, synthesize them, make some kind of sense. Writing is the best way for me to do that.

I have gotten a similar reaction, of being compelled to find out more, from every woman to whom I have shown the picture. "What's the story here? That's your *mom*?" Also interesting to me is that Elizabeth's Millenial-age friends have uniformly had the same reaction. I know they grew up watching *The Notebook*, so perhaps the image and story align with their ideas of romance. We all want to know who Mom was, and what happened to the lovers in that photograph.

It's strange to be equipped with only a few salient facts. I knew how their relationship started and why it had ended. I had an approximate timeframe for it—beginning in her senior year of high school. I knew my mother had gone on to quite a happy life.

But I needed more answers. Armed with the photographs, the two details my mother had mentioned, and my chats with Sally, I had my work cut out for me.

Sadly, Sally hadn't been able to remember Bill's last name, only that it was something "very traditional, very American." But I had these details: Bill had attended Penwell College, he was somewhere between one and three years older than my mom, his father was a minister, and he'd lived in one of the towns near Sally's grandparents, somewhere in southwestern Connecticut.

After those conversations with Sally, the next thing I planned to do was look through Mom's address book. Perhaps, like Pearl Tull, the matriarch in Anne Tyler's *Dinner at the Homesick Restaurant*, my mom had written down his address and updated it over the years. She knew he had become a teacher in Connecticut, so it was conceivable she'd tracked him down and they'd kept in touch. It was worth finding out.

The problem was, I had no idea where to find the address book. Mom had lived in that house for twenty-five years, the last four of which she had spent in declining physical and cognitive health. Many of the things that used to be in perfect order, like her financial files, had been scribbled over or commingled with old magazines and newspapers. At first, her computer had sticky notes with passwords crossed out and rewritten and phone numbers for every time she logged herself out accidentally; after the first year of her decline, she stopped using the computer altogether.

When Mom assigned me power of attorney, I made my best effort to secure significant documents, such as her deed and insurance policies, Social Security and Medicare cards, her birth and wedding certificates. I had smuggled out some specific rare photos. Not knowing how much the dementia would progress, I worried she might someday come across something and mistreat it, not understanding what it was, so I had been removing the most important things. Had I left the hand-written address book on its usual shelf in her kitchen? Was it somewhere else in the house? Had I already taken it away?

I searched through her office desk, her kitchen desk, and her bedside table, hoping to find the well-worn book. Nothing. I worried that I'd missed a great opportunity to unearth valuable information.

When I got back to my also-cluttered office, I went through various boxes of documents and photographs I had brought over "for safekeeping." I found her passport, the cemetery plot information for her and my dad, the folder full of wedding announcements and obituaries of the many people she had known over the years.

I went to bed that night disappointed in myself. I needed to look harder. There might be such a simple clue in her phone book, if only I could find it.

I woke up early the next morning and dove into the boxes in my office marked "Mom." Near the bottom of a plastic bin, under some old email printouts, was the address book.

It seemed smaller than I remembered. It was well-worn and full of cross-outs and updates from at least thirty years of changes. I felt some relief in finding it, yet I had no idea where to begin. I had no clue about Bill's last name, other than the fact that it was "traditional." Was he an Abbott or a Yates? And even if I knew his last name, she might have put his information anywhere, B for Bill or X for ex-boyfriend. I had no idea. I was going to have to go line by line through the entire address book, including the front and back panels of each divider where she'd scrawled additional notes.

I started to pore over the contents. He'd lived in Connecticut, so I looked for addresses with CT or phone numbers that began with a 203 area code. So many memories came up: old friends and associates of my mom and dad's, cousins who had since passed away. There was a whole page devoted to various doctors, none of whom she'd seen in at least a year.

Most of the names and addresses were written in ink. The most frustrating part was finding spots where I could see faint pencil marks—an indication that something written had since been erased. There were indentations sometimes, or smudges, but nothing intelligible. I had no idea whether there had once been some useful information…useful for my search, anyway.

Mom's friends had lived in all sorts of places: New York and Maryland, but also North Carolina, Florida, California, Illinois. I wasn't seeing much "Connecticut." There were a few Nutmeg State people, those I'd known for years from when my father was at Yale or cousins who lived in the general area, but I didn't come across any listing tied to an unfamiliar name.

I considered that it would have been too easy to look in her phone book and have his name and address jump off the page. I'd have to do more work, try something else.

At this early stage, the sole person who knew about my quest other than Sally was Elizabeth, the "snoop" who had found the photos in the first place. She was as intrigued as I was, and equally insistent that we had to find out more about Bill. I explained that the address book had been a dead end. I was going to look at Mom's old email files next, but I had a suspicion that that would also be fruitless.

Chapter 7
Not Left Behind

I couldn't stop thinking about how, even with a great marriage, my mother still kept those photos as she moved around from house to house. She had moved from her childhood apartment in New York to *eight* different homes over forty-two years since marrying my father. She'd had the opportunity many times to get rid of the box and its contents, yet she held onto it. Had she remembered what was in it? Had she opened it from time to time, had she ever considered not bringing it with her? These photos had even survived a major housecleaning purge, fifteen years ago, after the basement flooded. Not only had Mom kept them, but they resided in a secure and coveted spot on her bedroom bookshelf.

She could not have been unaware that at some point, after her passing, someone might discover the cache. I mean, yes, on the one hand, she put the pictures in a puzzle box because she didn't want them to be casually looked at, but she didn't get rid of them. What does that mean? Did she want them to be found? I'd like to think there was some intention involved. I can understand that she didn't want to lose them entirely; they were a part of her past. I have no idea how many times she went back to look inside the box over the years, possibly never, but it was still with her. Like her childhood panda, the contents were never thrown away.

I believed the girl in that picture deserved for her story to be told.

There were also things of mine she'd kept from move to move. Mom and Dad had relocated five times since I graduated from high school, over forty years ago, but she always held on to my archives. The collection wasn't just one little cigar box with a few photos. It was a big packing box full of letters, diaries, newspaper clippings, photos, autograph books, scripts, programs, awards. I had always kept my yearbooks with me, but I'd left this box full of memorabilia with my parents as they moved up and down the Northeast Corridor.

Periodically, my mother would ask, "Are you ever going to take back your stuff?" but she never demanded it or threatened to throw that box out, which I appreciated. I knew that someday I'd want to look at everything again.

In the midst of the ongoing search for Bill, I finally brought these archives back to my own house. Elizabeth considered the challenges we were facing and said she wanted to go through my box of memorabilia with me. She knew that someday I wouldn't be around to explain each item. She wanted to hear about my past directly from me, rather than have to figure it out by herself.

We had a lot of fun looking through it together. In fact, we had to go through the box over a couple of days because there was so much in there. Some things would provoke a smile or a "huh," others would warrant an extended anecdote or two.

This is a letter from a friend from camp, we were pen pals during the school year. My cousin and I visited her once, and her older school friends came over; we sat off to the side while they smoked pot in the basement. We felt super awkward...

This was the script from a play I was in, back in ninth grade. I had maybe three lines. The girl who played my sister is now a professional actress...

I can't believe I saved this lip gloss—in seventh grade I went to the mall every weekend with my friend. We used to get lunch at Woolworth's and buy records, candy bars, and lip gloss. Everyone gave each other Bonne Bell Lip Smackers or Life Savers Storybooks as Christmas presents.

Even now, I'm thinking about things that *weren't* in my box. I have no idea what happened to the pictures I used to have. There was never anything quite as compelling as the one I found of Mom, but there were plenty of old boyfriends in my life, old friends with inside jokes that I remembered after forty or fifty years, fun memories I was happy to share with Elizabeth to give her a little more insight into who I am.

Over the years, my mom sometimes voiced her opinions about my boyfriends, current and past. Sometimes an old beau achieved legendary status with my parents because of just how ridiculous he was: too conservative, or spacey, or awkward and buffoonish. "Your dad and I would laugh when he left the room," she said of one, after things had ended. Another time, she did me a huge favor by telling a guy I'd met at a youth dance that I wasn't home, and to please stop calling.

She never seemed enthusiastic about whomever I was currently dating, including the various "-steins" and "-bergs." But of all the guys, ever, she clearly had a favorite. Mom often talked about a boy I "went with" when I was in ninth grade. He was Irish, with dimples and green eyes. We've stayed friends over the years, and I have told him that my mother still talked about his green eyes, forty years later. In hindsight, maybe he reminded her of Bill.

Chapter 8
Penwell Archives

The address book had been a dead end. I needed to think of other ways to track Bill down. Sally said he had grown up near Fairfield, that his father was a minister, and he had attended Penwell. I also had photos. I decided to start with the Penwell clue.

My first thought was to ask for assistance from a second cousin whose son had graduated from Penwell a few years ago. I saw on the college website that all graduates have access to the alumni database, and I thought I might impose on him to do a quick search of guys named William who had attended the college between 1950 and 1956. Granted, there could be dozens, if not hundreds, but I had to start somewhere.

I asked my cousin if he thought his son would be willing to "help me out with a little sleuthing." My cousin said he would ask, but the son claimed no knowledge of such a database. Even though I knew a link was listed on the Penwell website, I decided to let the request go. I would continue my search via different methods.

I typed "Penwell Class of 1956" into Google, and the first thing that came up was a link to something about their sixty-fifth reunion. I decided to see what that might include: A list of names? Photographs? Mini biographies? It was worth a try.

The site revealed only the activities that took place at the most recent reunion, including lectures, concerts, and dinners, plus the alumni challenge to donate to a class gift. The reality was that Bill would have been something like eighty-seven at the sixty-fifth reunion, which was held during COVID. The chances of his involvement were not great.

But I persevered, typing in "Penwell commencement 1956," and found that the college had kept archives, including the program from the graduation ceremony. Would I have to go up to the college to view it? Fortunately, there were materials online, including a PDF of the actual program.

I hadn't realized how large the class was: over 350 people graduated that day. Penwell was already co-ed at the time, which eliminated a hundred students for me. I reviewed the list of names, noting any Williams I could find.

Between the bachelor of arts, bachelor of science, and combined degree programs, there turned out to be fifteen Williams. Sally had said that Bill's last name sounded traditionally American, so I eliminated anyone with a distinctly ethnic name like "DeCecco" or "Feldman." Of the names that remained, the most promising were "Clayton," "Madison," and "Whitehall."

I ran those by Sally, and she said, "I'm not sure, but Madison sounds possible."

I reflected for a moment. William Madison, or Billy Madison, was a famous name thanks to Adam Sandler's movie. I also had a friend from college, a writer named Bill Madison, who hailed from Texas. I was amused by the idea of that also being the name of my mother's lost love.

I began to think of the guy in the picture as "the other Bill Madison." I was going to need further corroboration. The next step was to use one of my other facts, as provided by Sally.

Chapter 9
Meanwhile, on Planet Earth

You may well ask, "What else was going on at this time, as you sifted through address books and commencement lists? Had you started taking care of your mother's affairs, contacted the creditors and utility companies one does after a funeral? Did you run an estate sale?"

To be honest, my mother passed away at a horrendous time.

Almost two years prior, in November of 2021, my mother-in-law, Sue, was diagnosed with pancreatic cancer, the same incurable disease that had taken her own mother, Bess—for whom Elizabeth was named—over thirty-five years earlier. The diagnosis was even tougher because Sue was completely lucid. She had always been a real dynamo, a working mother and a flawless homemaker. Nothing ever seemed to stop her. While she stoically wanted to undergo chemotherapy to prolong her life, she knew her days were limited.

Her biggest concern was not for her own health; she worried about her husband, Ken, a sweet, gentle man who had been receding into himself more and more over the past ten years. He was never diagnosed with a specific kind of dementia; he just stopped speaking. Over time, he also lost his ability to live as he once did. It was terrible watching a man who used to do the Sunday *Times* crossword in pen, an MIT-educated physicist who watched *Jeopardy!* every night, become less himself and more a hollow shell. He sometimes chimed in with a comment, but in the "before times," he had been incredibly quick-witted and loquacious. It was like hearing an echo, or seeing a ghost, of what he had once been.

Sue's greatest fear was leaving him alone in the world. She hated to think of what would become of him once she was gone. She and I became much closer during those two years. I tried all sorts of strategies to keep her spirits (and weight!) up. Other people were serious with her, but I did my best to be breezy and optimistic. I tried to reassure her by scouting out local assisted-living and memory-care places for Ken. Armed with that information, she finally settled on a few options from which she could choose, if and when she was no longer able to take care of him. She was determined to forestall that for as long as possible.

To make matters worse, this was all happening during the pandemic. Our three family seniors—my mother and my in-laws—got their first COVID vaccinations in February of 2021, and we did our best to keep them safe and current with all their shots, including flu. Although I came to see my mother several times a week, I visited my in-laws far less frequently to keep a protective "bubble" for Mom. We always masked unless we were sitting outside.

Despite our best attempts to keep them safe, both of my in-laws contracted COVID in early November 2022, a year into Sue's cancer treatment. They were able to take Paxlovid, but my father-in-law never fully recovered. The virus exacerbated his confusion, and he experienced a kidney infection that became septic.

All of our hesitance and concern about keeping apart from Ken and Sue evaporated. Elizabeth was at the hospital almost every day, tag-teaming with the rest of us—she was with Ken the first night, in the emergency room, when his blood pressure plummeted and he almost died. He developed complications from the infusions and antibiotics, including atrial fibrillation. His pulse and blood pressure were out of control. There were times during Ken's hospitalization when it wasn't clear whether he'd ever leave intensive care.

The doctors found there was nothing more they could do for him, so after three weeks he was moved to a rehab facility / nursing home. It was nothing like the memory-care places I had pre-screened; Ken's abilities were too limited and his needs too extreme for that sort of environment. He was also placed in residential care for my mother-in-law's well-being, so that she would not exhaust herself doing everything for him while she simultaneously underwent daily targeted radiation treatment. She insisted on sitting by his side, ten hours a day, at the nursing home. Sadly, Ken succumbed to his various complications in late January of 2023.

It might sound awful, but Sue no longer had to worry about what would become of Ken in her absence. In a way, it brought her true peace of mind. Her radiation treatments were successful in limiting the tumor's spread and gave her a few months free of chemotherapy. She had a good run of strong appetite and the most energy since her diagnosis. Unfortunately, the cancer soon came raging back, and by September, as my mom was declining, I could see my mother-in-law was becoming much weaker as well.

Simultaneously, we had the tremendous misfortune of my husband's spine reaching its breaking point. Well, not breaking, but he had terrible pain from a bulging disk. It was significant enough that he could barely walk. Just as my mother was beginning hospice care,

Michael became bedridden except for trips to an orthopedist and pain specialist.

Mom began hospice on a Wednesday. I met with the hospice nurse, hoping to smooth the transition, but it did not go well. The nurse asked Mom things like, "What year is it?" and "Who is the President?" to perform a cognitive assessment.

My mother replied, "What kind of a stupid question is that? Go away. What stupid questions you're asking!" Mom had no patience for her at all, and honestly, these were the least rude comments she made.

The nurse tried again. "Look, Karen's here!" she said, cheerfully.

My mother angrily spat out, "So what?"

I had long ago accepted that I would not be able to predict, from moment to moment, what kind of mood she would be in. All I could do was laugh. I said, "Thanks, Mom."

I needed to leave soon after, to go back home to take care of my husband. Michael's demands were exhausting me: just helping him get clean, dressed, medicated, and fed took almost two hours, and then we had to figure out a way to get him downstairs for the day. I tried to make him as comfortable as possible so that he might get through a half hour of work, or a phone call.

Finally, three days later (a Saturday), I made sure he was fed and comfortable in front of the television so I could take a quick trip over to Mom's to see how she was faring with the hospice treatment.

What I saw wasn't great. Mom seemed depleted, without energy. She hardly lifted her head when I came into her room. She had been moved to the twin-size bed the hospice had supplied, with its rails and adjustable lifts. It was a pathetic sight.

Dementia goes in only one direction, and she had been declining for many years. The final impetus for Mom to begin hospice was that she had ceased walking independently. For over a year, I had arranged twice-weekly physical therapy visits in the hope she would remain mobile, but it became too difficult for her to move or stand upright, even with a rollator or walker. It had also become impossible for her two live-in aides, Benta and Mercy, to change her clothing and linens in her usual king-size bed; the hospice equipment was much easier for them to work with, and we did what we could with soft pillows and sheets to make her comfortable there.

As had become her pattern over the past two years, Mom asked me, several times, what she needed to do that day. "Do I have to get out of bed?" she groaned.

I reassured her that she did not. "Do you want anything to eat or drink?" I asked. "I can help you sit up, if you want food."

"I don't want anything," she said. "I just want to sleep."

I left her bedroom and found Benta, who was covering the daytime shift. "It seems like she's not doing very well," I said. "What do you think? Is she starting to fail?"

Benta was capable and calm, highly attuned to Mom's needs. She told me she thought Mom was just tired and that she was not in a hurry to leave us.

The next day, in the early afternoon, Benta phoned me—something she almost never did. "Please get here as soon as you can," she said.

I told Michael I couldn't do anything for him—he would have to wait a while because I needed to go check on my mother. I called my brother in Israel as I drove to Mom's house, explaining that it sounded like something serious was happening. He and I had discussed the do-not-resuscitate (DNR) policy several times, as part of Mom's hospice plan; knowing that her "old self" would not have been happy with her current situation, and that CPR would be an aggressive procedure, I did not plan to contact the local emergency medical services.

When I got to Mom's house, Mercy was waiting for me, while Benta was in the bedroom with my mom. Mercy explained that, together, they had brought Mom to the kitchen table to eat breakfast. Mom had been talking with them but then suddenly slumped over. She convulsed a few times, and they decided the safest place for her was back in the hospice bed. They returned her to her bedroom via the wheelchair, and that was when Benta called me.

I asked for a few minutes alone with Mom. I saw immediately that her eyes were wide open, her pupils dilated—she was unable to focus on any one thing. I tried to speak with her, but she couldn't respond. I recognized that she must have had a stroke; after years of TIAs (transient ischemic attacks, or mini strokes), she had suffered a major episode. I kept trying to get her to connect, to make eye contact, and for a moment I saw a spark of recognition. I knew she saw me.

Years ago, a good friend invited me to join an online support group for caregivers of dementia patients. Members offered invaluable advice, from initial stages through hospice and end-of-life situations. I learned from hundreds of other people's experiences that the important thing when someone reached the stage my mother now faced was to let her know she was loved, that she wasn't alone, but also that she was allowed to let go.

I remembered that advice, in the moment. "Mom, it's okay. I'm here with you now, everyone is fine, and we'll be okay if you have to go." I kept repeating that she had been a good mom, that I loved her, and it was okay for her to let go.

At one point she said, "Wha—wha—?" I realized she was, as ever, trying to ask me what she should be doing, and I said, "Just rest, Mom. Nobody's expecting you to do anything. You're a great mom, you're allowed to rest. I love you."

Perhaps a minute went by, and I realized she hadn't been breathing. I called both aides into the bedroom and said, "I can't tell—is she gone?"

Mercy checked her pulse and breathing, then gently closed Mom's eyelids and folded her hands. It was hard to believe, after all the stress of the past four years, that our final interaction had been so peaceful. We'd argued, we'd fought, I'd worn myself ragged worrying about all sorts of nonsense like utility bills and new medications and getting to appointments on time…and in the end, it was just so calm and simple.

I called my brother to let him know Mom had passed. He thought he could get a flight from Israel on Monday, and we could have the burial on Tuesday. Just for context, this was three weeks after the October 7, 2023 attacks by Hamas. My brother had seven grandchildren (including three under the age of one) and their mothers living in his house, since their fathers (one son and two sons-in-law) were performing military service. His oldest daughter, living about an hour away from him, was pregnant with her fourth child and due to deliver sometime that week. Even amid this chaotic situation, he and my sister-in-law arranged to come to the States.

I told my sister, then my husband and kids. I called hospice to send someone to certify the death. I called the funeral home to begin the preparations: ordering a casket, arranging for removal of Mom's body, and, ultimately, coordinating a graveside service and burial at the cemetery. I contacted the rabbi and cantor to schedule the actual time of the memorial service and to help plan what we would need for shiva, the Jewish ritual of mourning.

Jewish burial is expected to take place without delay—ideally, within twenty-four hours. The logistics keep you so busy, it's difficult to dwell on your loved one and the full impact of what has happened.

Elizabeth was with Sue when I called to tell her. We decided there was no way Sue would be able to attend the graveside service, wheelchair bound as she was. She expressed great regret and frustration about it. I told her I didn't think shiva would be a good idea either, as she would be risking exposure to COVID.

My husband was in the same situation, at least vis-à-vis being wheelchair bound. He couldn't leave the house, let alone get to the funeral, and would be unable to attend the shiva. I hired a live-in aide to stay with him while I handled the arrangements for the funeral and my siblings' comfort, as well as attending shiva every evening.

Aware of his own mother's decline, Michael feared he might not be able to say goodbye to her in person. Sue passed away at the end of the next week. In those twelve days between losing one mom and then the other, I was able to bring him down, with his wheelchair, to visit with her twice while she was still able to speak. It was a heartbreaking, exhausting time for everyone—worse for my kids, who had lost all three of their remaining, beloved grandparents in the span of ten months.

Perhaps now you can recognize how much of a gift it was to have this distraction—to embark upon this quest to know the secret of my mother's past. After four years of watching her nightmarish decline, the photos Elizabeth unearthed allowed me to see Mom as a vibrant young girl, in the throes of an exciting romance. I don't know many people who wouldn't seize on this opportunity to glimpse their mother's youth, to cling to this newly discovered chapter of her life as a chance to understand and appreciate her.

There were many moments that were both numbing and challenging: helping my husband with each daily task, setting up a house for shiva, taking "the Moms'" dry goods and unused health supplies to a food bank or packing up their clothing for donation. Then, of course, there was the financial responsibility of serving as my mother's executor, closing out her accounts, paying taxes, and arranging for the sale of her home.

I embraced the pursuit of this story, this ongoing mystery of the photographs, as something positive to be looked forward to and savored. Seeing this side of Mom brought joy, rather than despair. I'd already been dwelling in sorrow for four years, mourning first the ongoing loss of my mother, then witnessing Sue's decline from cancer. I will always miss them both, but I treasured discovering the previously unknown Ellen.

Chapter 10
Religion and Family

The anecdote Sally had shared about dining with Bill's parents was relatable. Mealtime is a rare opportunity for people of different generations to spend meaningful time together. That was even more true when I was growing up in the 1970s.

We lived far away from most of our cousins, many of whom were in the New York metropolitan area or on the West Coast. Multigenerational holiday dinners grew in importance because they were so rare. Dining with the whole clan was a significant occasion, a major event where important announcements were made about new jobs, college acceptances, health topics. One's presence at these gatherings lent legitimacy to relationships: you knew things were serious when your cousin brought a date to Thanksgiving dinner or a Passover seder.

Though I didn't grow up with a lot of Jewish ritual, I developed a real love for Friday night dinners during my senior year of high school, when my boyfriend's family welcomed me to their Shabbat table. I got to experience practical Judaism, the joy of being together, of taking time during a busy week to exist and celebrate. His mother gave me a set of candlesticks as a graduation gift, encouraging me to continue to celebrate Shabbat. I'll always be grateful for her warmth and generosity.

On the flip side, negative things sometimes come out at the dinner table. We've all heard about the drunk uncle who says inappropriate, politically incorrect things at a holiday gathering. Sometimes it's the little brother who reveals an awkward family secret, or an older sister who brings up a "cute story" that somehow includes nudity. You often find out more than you'd bargained for.

Back in the mid-1980s, a Jewish friend of mine told me a story about an uncomfortable dinner she had with her college boyfriend's family. He came from a large Irish American family and had invited her to his home in Upstate New York for the weekend. About halfway through the meal, his brothers teased their youngest sister about her current boyfriend. They pretended to have no respect for him.

"Eh, I guess he's not so bad," said one of the brothers. "I mean, he's Italian, but at least he's Catholic."

My friend said she felt like throwing up. She didn't appear traditionally Jewish, and she wasn't even sure if her boyfriend knew that she wasn't Christian, but to hear things spelled out so clearly was something she had not expected. She said their relationship ended almost as soon as they got back to campus; ever since that dinner, she had been dreading the moment when the other shoe would drop, when she would be "exposed."

Another friend related that when his Polish Catholic mother fell in love with his Italian Catholic father in 1952, her parents told her they would give only $100 to the couple for their new home. "But if you marry Tomasz (another suitor who had emigrated from Poland), we'll give you $500!" Fortunately, she persevered despite the smaller gift.

This kind of stratification is common within subcultures. Caste; having "good hair," the right skin tone, or a certain body type; being a Mayflower descendant, in the Social Registry or a Daughter of the American Revolution; going to the right schools—all of these are distinctions within larger groups, standards to make one feel included or excluded.

There have been similar intra-Jewish issues. The pecking order within Jewish American subcommunities has changed over time. The German Jews who crossed the Atlantic in the 1840s-1870s paid their dues like every other immigrant group. Some rose, some fell. Many gave up their rituals and assimilated as much as possible. German Jewish professionals and businesspeople settled all over the country, from Manhattan to San Francisco, before a second major pogrom- and conscription-fueled wave of Jewish immigrants came from Eastern Europe, circa the 1880s-1920.

German Jews looked down on the recently-arrived "greenhorns," more religiously observant fellow Ashkenazim (European Jews), but those Germans weren't even the first Jews in America. Sephardim (Jews who had resettled from the Iberian Peninsula or North Africa) arrived on the continent in 1650, settling in New Amsterdam, two hundred years before the Germans. Toward the end of the second wave of immigration, even more Sephardic Jews came from Greece, Syria, and Turkey.

From 1930 onward, Jews fleeing Europe tried desperately to come to the US. Some ended up in Canada, Cuba, South America, South Africa, Australia, even China. There was always someone "newer" who yearned for acceptance.

As I mentioned earlier, my mother's father, Jeff, could trace his American roots to the mid-1800s, including the ancestor who served in the Union Army during the Civil War. Jeff's wife, the notorious Estelle, unhesitatingly took on a mantle of prominence via his German surname. She dreaded appearing too Jewish. She spoke of her

American childhood in Waterbury, Connecticut, playing football with her brothers. She distanced herself as much as possible from immigrants on the Lower East Side of Manhattan.

My father's heritage was steeped in that "lesser" Lower East Side background. Dad's paternal grandfather emigrated from the Pale of Settlement—that region of the Russian empire (now Poland, Ukraine, and Belarus) where, for about 125 years, Eastern European Jews were permitted to live. He worked as a pushcart peddler, but his sons lived the early-twentieth-century American dream: my grandfather, George, earned a law degree and specialized in intellectual property / copyright law in music publishing. His brother, my great-uncle Lou, managed the Andrews Sisters, the most popular female vocal group of the 1940s. Lou brought a Yiddish folk tune to Sammy Cahn and Saul Chaplin, asking them to write the English lyrics that became "Bei Mir Bist du Schön," the girls' first major hit. He also supplied other performers with successful songs in the 1950s and 1960s.

My father's mother, Sarah, was the daughter of a rabbi who emigrated from Latvia. She was the first in her family to be born in America—raised in Paterson, New Jersey, before moving to Manhattan and meeting George at a settlement house, a community resource and occasional social club for Jewish immigrant families. Sarah's father—the last in a long family line of rabbis from Riga—was reluctant to have his eldest daughter marry a less religious man, but she and George were very much in love. At least the groom studied law; that must have been a consolation. Sarah made sure that each of her two sons studied to become a bar mitzvah.

I was raised closer to Estelle's ideal: Sunday school (no Hebrew) and occasional Hanukkah candles, a Christmas tree and Easter baskets. I'm sure my father didn't broadcast the latter information to his mother.

My siblings and I still carry genes from our great-grandfather, the rabbi. Despite lacking a formal American Jewish childhood education, my brother became a *ba'al teshuvah*, a more observant Jew. He and his wife made *aliyah*, raising their five children in Israel. One of his sons is a rabbi. My sister and I both married Jewish men, sent our kids to Hebrew day school, and are affiliated with the Conservative Jewish movement.

I'd say Estelle would be rolling in her grave to find out all of this, but that would be impossible. In violation of Jewish law, she was, of course, cremated.

Chapter 11
Love and Memory

Concurrent with this search for the mystery boyfriend, I was intrigued in the abstract about my mother's romantic past and Bill's prominence in her history. Mom had alluded that their romance ended because of religious differences. She met my father about two years later, after her sophomore year.

In the interim, Mom, a Barnard girl, went on dates with Columbia boys. She referred to them en masse. In later years, well after my father died and she joined our synagogue for social reasons, she recognized a name in the directory and said, "I dated him once at Columbia. Hmm." She seemed uninterested in getting reacquainted with him; I doubt they ever spoke of it. It seemed indicative of most romantic entanglements she had in those two interim years: date a guy once or twice, move on. Nothing appeared to have been serious, except that Columbia junior to whom she "got pinned" during her sophomore year—but she seemed not at all conflicted about ending it with him as soon as she met my dad.

Yet, speaking of moving, I still marveled at the fact that she had carried Bill with her in her thoughts, and most tangibly, in that puzzle box. I don't imagine she pined for him, opening it up daily or anything. She might not have even looked inside the box once she put away the photos, yet she never culled it from her possessions. Eight different moves, as well as a complete purge of old files, and she never threw it away.

Although I'm not sure he knew about the pictures, I believe my dad knew about Bill. Mom had mentioned dating someone who wasn't Jewish, and how it ended because of that, in the context of trying to comfort me when my own interfaith relationship ended. My father's comment: "Well, you've had your heart broken, now you're ready to settle down," feels like it echoes back to a story he heard three decades earlier. Like mother, like daughter, we had to go through failed romances before finding "Mr. Right".

That must be why I said "poor Mom" when Elizabeth told me about the photos. Poor Mom—even after seventy years, she still held a special place for Bill in her heart. And yet, she had that great relationship with my dad. Love is a complicated thing, and first love is intense. I can't imagine she ever regretted choosing my dad, but there was a piece of her that was never going to forget Bill.

Even as I write that sentence, I have to laugh. With her dementia, so many things fell away. She forgot that my sister had passed twenty years ago. She couldn't remember how my father died, and later on she couldn't remember that he had died, at all. On those rare times she asked where he was, I would tell her he was out getting gardening supplies.

She forgot about the day-to-day administration she had done for so many years. I guess she took me at my word when I told her I would handle everything; she stopped worrying. In prior years,

I remember going with her to the post office to send every IRS check via certified mail, and to the township office to hand-deliver her quarterly property taxes. Once I had assumed responsibility for her tax-paying and accounting, she never dwelled on it. I remember mentioning once that it was April 15, and she didn't react at all.

A different year, I said, "I've been busy filing taxes."

She replied, "It's a good thing I don't work, so I don't have any income."

"You're right, Mom," I said, recalling the advice to meet her where she was. Don't argue. Sometimes it was challenging to not react.

Like most people with dementia, she also got confused about time. She watched the same two Gene Kelly movies, as well as the Gordon MacRae version of *Oklahoma!*, nearly every day. She asked me if Gene Kelly was still alive, and I said, "I don't think so." She looked at her daily schedule one day and said, "February 9, why does that date sound familiar?" and I said that it was Estelle's birthday—she would have been 123 years old that day. My mom asked, "Should we call her?"

Knowing that she hadn't remembered what happened to my sister or my dad, it was possible that in those last few years she forgot Bill. She still remembered her friend Sally, and she remembered my kids when she saw them. She wasn't so good with specific facts. I could tell her five times in an hour that Elizabeth was at law school, or that my son had just performed in a nightclub, and she'd say, "That's wonderful. So, what's going on with your kids?"

Her ninety-one-year-old brother, who lived on the West Coast, came to surprise her during a post-vaccine lull in June of 2022. She lit up like a light bulb, she was so happy to see him, and was more "herself" than she had been in some time. Their goodbye at the Amtrak station was bittersweet, at least for me, being the only one who was aware this would likely be the last time they'd be together. As soon as we left the station, Mom didn't recall any of the visit. I showed her photos, and I had taken some videos I replayed for her for weeks afterward. She enjoyed watching them, although she always seemed surprised that they both had white hair.

It's been said that you don't necessarily remember what people say, but you never forget how they made you feel. I have to believe that's what we're talking about here—that Mom may have forgotten the specifics about whether certain people were alive or gone, but she always knew that she loved them.

Chapter 12

Son of a Preacher Man

As I eased into the next stage of sleuthing, I reviewed the key facts in my possession: the sweatshirt Bill wore in the photo meant he'd attended Penwell, Sally said he'd grown up near Fairfield, Connecticut, and his father was a minister. I decided to follow up on the Fairfield minister lead, to find out the surnames of clergy from that era and whether any matched those of the Williams who had graduated from Penwell; I was specifically hoping to find a "Madison."

There were at least four or five neighboring towns, plus Fairfield itself, to explore. I did internet searches on each one, looking for Christian denominational churches (other than Catholic). Some of the churches had developed different cultural constituencies in the past seventy years—for instance, holding services in Korean or Spanish, but I decided to try all of them.

I focused on clergy who officiated in the early 1950s, when my mother was still in high school, and drafted a preliminary letter I could email. I first verified, by their websites, that each congregation had been in existence in the 1950s. That eliminated a quarter of them. I ended up with a list of nine.

The original email read:

Hi, I'm doing some research and was wondering if you could provide me with the names of any clergy that worked at the church between 1952 and 1956. Thank you.

Looking at it now, I realize I should have started from the 1940s up until 1953, but in any event, I hit send and waited to see what kind of response I got.

Only one minister replied. He explained that there had been a single clergyman in charge throughout the forties and fifties, with certain ministerial trainees coming in for a year or two each during that timeframe. I knew Bill's father would have been too old to be a trainee, and the chief minister's last name wasn't Madison.

I didn't want to make a bunch of phone calls, and I couldn't see myself driving up to the Fairfield area to go through church archives. I decided that, while the church angle was salient, it was not going to be the most fruitful way of finding Bill. I had to consider a different approach.

Chapter 13
New Developments

Even after the tumult of two shivas had come and gone, I still had my hands full, balancing my attempt to help Michael with trying to console my two kids, who had just lost three of the most important people in their world. Everyone was hurting, and even though I had this secret project that made me happy, I knew I needed to focus on the here and now.

We were fortunate to have a neighbor who is a doctor of physical therapy. He connected us with a surgeon who would be fixing Michael's herniated disk as soon as we could get approval from the insurance company. In the meantime, I was trying to keep my husband from abject misery. He was accustomed to exercising six days a week, and the thought that he could barely make it up and down a flight of stairs, once a day, was something we had never planned for. I didn't know what would happen if the surgery failed. I tried to help him eat healthily, but perhaps I was a little too cautious about caloric intake. Because of his inactivity, he lost twenty pounds of muscle mass in the span of weeks.

Michael had surgery right before Thanksgiving and recovered over that weekend. It was the third year in a row we'd had a terrible holiday: in 2021, Sue was in the hospital for complications and, to explain her absence, we had to tell the kids about her recent cancer diagnosis; in 2022, both Ken and Sue had COVID, so we waved to them from the hallway of their apartment building. Here we were in 2023, with no grandparents at all. The only conceivable bright spot was that the spine surgery seemed to be successful, although the surgeon warned that recovery could take up to four months.

I still thought about the puzzle box project when I could. I was talking about it with my therapist, explaining that I had failed to get responses from the churches and that I wished I had more information from the Penwell lead. She said, "What about a yearbook? You can compare the name to the photo."

What *about* a yearbook? I didn't think it would be worth driving five hours to see the campus archives, but perhaps, like everything else in the world, it might be available online. I did an eBay search and, voilà! The 1956 Penwell College Yearbook, available for only $48, including shipping.

It wasn't a trivial sum of money, but I figured it might be just the thing to help me solve the mystery. I ordered it and waited patiently in the hope I'd get at least some of my questions answered.

About ten days later, I had my very own copy of the 1956 yearbook. It contained no autographs or personal markings at all.

Just as I had with the commencement program, I began looking through the names. The Williams were few and far between, and when I got to William Madison, I could see that he was not our guy. This William Madison was dark haired and heavyset. He looked like he might have played football. Our Bill was fair and slim, at least as a freshman. There was no way his appearance would have changed that dramatically in three years.

I looked at all the other Williams in the class of 1956. None of them looked a thing like the happy friend of my mother's. Perhaps he hadn't had a graduation picture taken. Perhaps he had graduated early. Perhaps he had transferred to a different college. It was clear the William I sought was not in this yearbook.

I decided to take a gamble and tracked down the 1955 yearbook, as well. This would have made him as much as three years older than my mom, and I wasn't too keen on that thought—but I was committed to my research and wanted to be sure I had explored every possibility.

While I was waiting for the second yearbook to arrive, Elizabeth went up to Boston to spend a birthday weekend with some law school classmates. The topic of her recent loss of grandparents came up, with friends offering condolences, and she shared the story about finding the photos. The women, all in their late twenties, were intrigued, and bombarded her with questions. They wanted to know everything we'd learned so far. It was obvious this story had legs.

When the second yearbook arrived, I was equally disappointed. It didn't contain the Bill we knew. I looked through all the Williams, and boy oh boy, there were some unattractive guys at Penwell. Maybe it was their hairstyles, or the fact that there wasn't as much orthodontia back then, but *yikes*. I began to think twice about what I'd said about my "goofy" dad; compared to these guys, he was just fine.

Chapter 14
A Familiar Story

Just like Elizabeth, as I'd been sharing the story with friends, every woman had been intrigued. Sometimes they shared parallel stories.

I spoke with my second cousin, Jenna, whose mom was one of my mother's favorite cousins and had lived independently well into her eighties. After her mother passed at age ninety-three, Jenna was cleaning out the assisted-living unit and came across an alligator-skin suitcase. It was only after her passing that my cousin ever saw the case or its contents.

"She had saved love letters from several old boyfriends. This was during World War II, when the younger men were away, fighting. It was the slightly older men who wrote her letters and courted her."

The most fascinating part, Jenna explained, was that three different men wrote about their plans to visit her mother at a lake resort where she would be staying for three weeks. It sounded like something out of Feydeau, with the possibility of her having to duck one and then another guy while she spent time with the third.

The irony was that it was on this vacation that she met her husband.

"Even so, even with a long and happy marriage, she kept those letters all those years, and even brought them with her to the assisted-living facility," Jenna marveled.

Elizabeth and I tried to imagine the shoe on the other foot, and what might have happened if we found old photos of my father's girlfriends. It's certainly possible those were among the things that my mom had purged during one of their moves, or in the clean-out after he passed away. I will never know. One thing I do know about my father's old girlfriends is that he was quite a "player" before he met my mom, something I found out in an unexpected way.

In 1975, my dad's brother began sending my cousins to the same summer camp he and Dad had attended as children. The camp owner contacted my dad. "Why aren't you sending your kids, too?"

Dad explained, as he often did, that he was raising four kids on a government salary.

The camp owner said, "Sign them up. I'll take care of the fees."

My sisters and I started there the following summer. One rainy day, killing time in the administrative building, I was browsing through old camp newspapers from the time of Dad's tenure. To my surprise, there was an article about a play featuring my father and two girls from his age group, one named Karen and the other, Jojo. From the day she was born, that was my sister's nickname; she only used "Joanne" professionally. I knew there was no way it was a coincidence. When I confronted my father with the newspaper story, he blushed.

So, how would another person feel, coming across photos of their father with an old girlfriend? Each woman I talked to was much more enthusiastic about her mother's past life. She didn't want to know about her dad's old flames—didn't want to hear he had ever been serious with another girl before finding her mom.

A mother having an interesting past, on the other hand, seems to be universally intriguing and romanticized.

"I'm glad she didn't settle down right away."

"She was so pretty."

"She was happy."

I think we like the idea—if it was a happy marriage—that our moms chose our dads. That they'd had autonomy and independence, a chance to see the world before settling down. We wanted to think they had made the right choice, to believe they'd even had a choice in the first place.

Chapter 15
Whither Truth?

S oon after the second yearbook fizzled, I despaired of ever finding Bill. He had not been in the yearbook for 1955 or 1956. As I speculated, he might have dropped out of Penwell, or transferred halfway through. Maybe he just didn't sit for a senior portrait. Regardless, the trail had gone cold.

I knew I still had things to say about my mom and how much all this deep sleuthing had helped me with the grieving process. From the moment I saw that photo of my mom on Bill's lap, I felt this was a tale worth telling.

I am a journalist by nature—I know a good story when I see or hear it, and I find out answers through interviews and research. I prefer to have facts, rather than guesses. I didn't want the story to be artificial; "unbelievable" and "incredible" were not my goals.

This story fascinated me, on many levels, but I wasn't sure how to write it with one of the two main characters being a cipher. I would not be able to pass *New Yorker* fact-checker levels of verification without knowing more about Bill, and I wasn't sure whether I could, or even should, go ahead with my writing without every detail.

I realized that I had a lot to say beyond their simple, yet mysterious tale of courtship. Mom had kept those memories for many years, but had a happy, successful, albeit too-brief marriage with someone else. At no point during Mom's life or after the discovery of those photos had I ever once doubted the strength of my parents' marriage. They were a great couple, totally devoted to one another and, as I inscribed on her headstone, "best friends."

That said, the story touched on many other topics. The romance was an exciting and interesting draw, of course, but I also wanted to consider the historical context of interfaith dating and marriage, and how it had evolved in the past seventy years; caregiving for someone with dementia in the time of COVID; and finding a healthy way to cope with loss. It seemed like I had a fertile subject for a kind of memoir, even if I didn't have all the facts.

I decided to work harder on the other aspects of research, and to speculate about those things I couldn't verify. Perhaps Bill would simply be a metaphor, a symbol of Mom's youth and her attempt to forge a life and self-image separate from Estelle.

Chapter 16

Widening the Circle

A fog lifted for Michael and me at the end of the year. About five weeks after his surgery, he'd made significant strides in his recovery. For example, he no longer took pain medication, was able to dress himself, and worked at his desk for hours at a time.

When he mentioned he had scheduled a follow-up appointment with his surgeon, I chastised him for not clearing it with my calendar, too. He said, "I'll be driving myself, and I can walk fine. I won't need you to push me in a wheelchair."

I was stunned. The caregiving for my mother had been immediately replaced by the caregiving for my husband, and I hadn't considered that it could end, that a person could improve and resume independence. I felt my stress dissipate. We decided to take a daytrip to New York City, something we hadn't done in months between worrying about our mothers and his injury.

We were eating lunch at Mercado Little Spain in Manhattan, and I felt happy being back out in the world again. I asked, "What would you think about taking a trip to Paris this spring?" He loves travel as much as, if not more than, I do—certainly in the years of caregiving, he encouraged me to get away, but I felt overwhelmed with obligations.

He jumped at my proposition. We began discussing plans for a week-long trip, including taking the "Chunnel" to London.

At last, after two months, I also told him about the photos and my plan to write a book. I talked of how it had kept me sane while I was caring for him, a special project I could think about and feel enthusiasm for, even as I was helping him with climbing the stairs, bathing and dressing, and shlepping his walker, water bottles, pillows, chargers, and snacks. It was difficult serving as caregiver for a sentient, normally active person who was frustrated, in pain, and unused to being disabled. I was fortunate to have had a place where I could go, mentally, to get a much-needed boost of energy.

I had also kept him out of the loop because I didn't think he would be interested in the topic. My assessment was correct: he wasn't critical of the idea, and in fact he was pleased to see me motivated about writing again, but the story itself didn't resonate with him.

There was another person with whom I hadn't yet discussed the photos, someone I knew would be far more receptive and would share my enthusiasm. I got my opportunity to communicate with her a couple of weeks later when I was clearing out more items from my mother's house.

Born in 1990, only three weeks after Estelle passed away, my oldest niece was given her great-grandmother's true birth name, Esther. She loves art, literature, and drama. She is a natural leader and has a career as a drama therapist, working with hospital patients. Esther lives in a hipster town in Israel, but I imagine she would feel right at home in any art colony—Santa Fe perhaps, or Woodstock, New York—someplace bohemian.

Esther delivered her fourth baby, a girl, five days after Mom passed away. My mother's given name, Ellen, means "bright one" or "shining light," and the new baby is named after her: "Oriyah," or "God's light." Oriyah is beautiful—a true Gerber baby. With so much going on at home, I knew Esther must be exhausted. I hadn't wanted to bother her.

I had been trying to allocate my mother's personal effects among her ten grandchildren. I took photos of her jewelry, and after appraisal found that most of it was semi-precious and costume stuff. I sent the pictures to my sister-in-law in Israel, asking which items her three daughters and two daughters-in-law might want.

Esther had said that she was only interested in my mother's purses and scarves, so I sent her those specific photos. We exchanged some comments back and forth on WhatsApp, and then I thought, "She really needs to hear about Mom. It would just make her day."

I sent her an email, making it clear I was trusting her with a secret and explaining that she was not to discuss my still-developing project with any of her siblings, parents, or my sister. I didn't include the photos with the email, as I knew they would be a huge distraction; plus, the suspense heightened the drama—something I knew she would appreciate.

Esther is well aware that my brother is much more religiously observant than I am, and that he might not be comfortable hearing about Mom's previous romantic life. I didn't want to upset him.

On the other hand, I told her, this opportunity was a reward for what I had been through, caring for my mom over these long years. More than any one tangible item, I saw this as her final gift to me, the opportunity to find a new way of knowing her. I wanted to work on my project without any conflict from my siblings—I planned to present the book as a fait accompli, when they would not be able to impede my flow.

I'm including her email response, verbatim. I considered it the ultimate validation and green light:

First of all, wow. Wow wow wow. I'm shocked and you are right this is definitely up my alley. I'm shocked and surprised but also moved, emotional even. Do those photos mean she wasn't the ol' grandma I knew? That there was more? Wow! Was this before or after grandpa? Or during?? So many questions.

I definitely want to see them and I CAN'T WAIT to read a book about what you think or know went down. Grandma was very, very precious to me and anything that can bring her to life especially parts I never knew about is in my opinion an absolute gem, a unique opportunity that can't be missed.

I definitely understand your need to keep it hush hush, creativity must be kept safe lest someone pisses it out when it's in the flickering light stage, and sometimes well after as well. I'm sure when you have the finished product it will be strong enough to stand on its own and withstand any disgruntlement or attempted interference. I trust your judgment completely and I definitely agree, you've earned this! And I think grandma deserves this story to be told, and by the best person of all to tell it, and that is you.

Thank you for sharing this with me. I feel so happy inside for some reason lol. I guess it makes me happy finding out how people always have layers, and are complicated and intricate and always uniquely themselves and in some way unknown to the world, but that it is possible to get to know many hidden pieces and go on loving.

Chapter 17
But Wait, There's More

After I read her email reaction, Esther and I continued the conversation on WhatsApp. She sent me the "exed-out eyes" emoji, saying she was "dead," that she was still in shock, and that this was such a juicy plot twist.

I told her to get ready for more shocks.

I began the slow photo reveal. First, I sent the two couples, which included the girl who turned out to be my mom's friend Sally.

I also sent the photo of just Mom and Mr. X, taken on the same afternoon, making it clear that he was her date.

Esther responded, "omg, who is heeeee?"

And I wrote, "So wait. Here's the one that made me say 'I have to write this book,'" and sent her the photo from the party.

"OMG I'm deaddd... If this book doesn't get written I'm FORC-ING you to write it... Who is that girl and who is that woman who kept the photos of those two, HIDDEN, for yearzzz?"

I told her that Elizabeth and I had been speculating that if a girl came across those photos of her grandfather, she'd say, "Oh, gross, why did Grandpa keep pictures of some other girl?" but when she finds it of her grandma she says, "Oh, yeah, tell mé more!"

Esther replied, "omg this is seriously too much, it's beyond my wildest imagination."

I wrote, "But wait, there's more. Are you ready for something that's going to shake your world? Elizabeth says this one is the biggest enigma."

Esther said, "Show me."

Reader, I have a confession to make. I've been withholding a salient fact that adds a new dimension to the story.

There were indeed four black-and-white photos in the box: the foursome in casual attire; just Mom and Bill; Mom and Bill dressed up at a party; and a picture of Bill relaxed and staring out into space, his hands behind his head.

You're about to get what Esther also got, in real time:

There was a fifth photo. A color photo. I couldn't quite place the year. I guessed that Bill was somewhere between forty-five and sixty years old, but it was most definitely him.

"*WHAAA—What? What? What?* I can't even handle it. When is this photo from? I'm just flabbergasted!"

I replied, "We. Don't. Know."

"Never in a million years."

When was it taken? Where was it taken? Who took it? How did it get to Mom? Did she see him in person? I had so many questions.

The fact that there was a more recent photo made it clear that the box was not a passive souvenir. My mother had added the color shot to her collection later in life, and intentionally kept the photos together. This materially changed the story. There was no question that the color photo was taken when Mom was…my mom. When she was an adult. It didn't look like it was from after my father died, since Bill was older than my dad and did not appear over sixty.

Mom was happily married to my dad then. Did she contact Bill? Did he contact her? What transpired?

Perhaps the photo was received at the same time she found out he was a high school teacher in Connecticut. After all, she mentioned she'd known that about him, and such information didn't materialize out of thin air.

"Esther, you don't know how much I wish there was an app or some genius somewhere who could analyze the photo and say, 'Oh, that sweater is from 1972,' or 1986, or whatever. I'm guessing he's anywhere between forty-five and sixty in that photo."

Talking with my niece reminded me of what I'd been going through earlier in my search. As we'd hit more and more dead ends in our pursuit of the young man in the photo, I told Elizabeth that I wished we knew a Kremlinologist. Perhaps I was using the term somewhat incorrectly, but to me that meant the kind of person who could take a tiny bit of information and extrapolate worlds from it. We've seen how a picture paints a thousand words. I know that a simple photograph can provide layers of information if you use analytical tools. Why else did all those spy gadgets include cameras?

My first exposure to the concept of Kremlinology was from a college friend who, when most of us were trying to decide if we were going to be writers or lawyers or doctors or teachers, announced he was studying Russian so he could do research and analysis for the State Department or the CIA. It had never dawned on me that such a career was possible.

I thought about what a photo can disclose. A viewer can sense the time period by what the people are wearing and their hairstyles; if you know at least one of the individuals, you can probably guess their age at the time of the photo. You can also make some assumptions based on the time of year and the activity they're engaged in, whether the setting is urban or rural, day or night, indoor or out-door. You can look at the expressions on their faces. Since this photo was from well before the days of digital cameras, there was only one shot, and so even if there were a few flubs or silly faces, it was still a realistic representation.

Sometimes you could tell where a photo was taken. Obvious-ly, if it wasn't in front of a national landmark or a restaurant or another clearly identifiable location, you had to do some inter-pretation. Was it a home, a classroom, a library, a garden, a train station, a store?

I wanted more information from the black-and-white shots than they were ever going to be able to show me. When were they taken exactly, and where? How long had Mom and Bill known each other? Was there more than one copy of each photo? Were there other photos taken, and who had those? And who was the photographer, anyway?

We had now brought Esther onto the team or "Ellen Fan Club," as Elizabeth called it. I half seriously asked whether my niece knew anyone in military intelligence who was good at this sort of thing. I mean, Mossad agents can track people by taking thirty-year-old snapshots and applying "aging" software to figure out what they might look like in present day. Maybe they could help us deter-mine Bill's approximate age in the color picture. Just from eye-balling it, I had placed his age as somewhere within a fifteen-year span, depending on whether he colored his hair and how quickly it was thinning. Other factors would be if he drank or smoked. I know from experience that there are old-looking forties and young-looking sixties out there.

As my mother's memory started declining, we printed names

and dates on the back of certain old pictures for her. Obviously, at that time, we were unaware of these particular photos, but in general I wish I had been more deliberate in taking down information. There are some black-and-white shots of her with her parents, or even with my dad, where it would have been nice to get some context. Now all I have are whatever stories I can recall and the clues I'm able to gather from what I see.

So, what did I see in the color portrait? The florid tone of Bill's skin showed that he was still active, not ghostly pale. He wore tinted aviator frames, and in the earlier image, he hadn't needed eyeglasses at all. Then again, neither had Mom in the 1950s. For as long as I'd known her, however, she'd worn them—I remember her wearing the "cat lady" kind in the late 1960s and early 1970s. Even twenty-five years older, with spectacles, he still had his delicate nose and protruding ears. His color picture was taken indoors, where he was surrounded by books. It could have been a school, a library, a bookstore, a home with lots of bookshelves.

He was wearing a heavy-knit sweater. It wasn't quite an ugly Christmas sweater. It had more natural tones than that, shades of brown and ivory, which again made me think late 1970s or early 1980s.

My father-in-law, who was only about three months younger than my mom, was still wearing the same clothes in 2020 that he'd worn all of his adult life. In the nearly thirty-three years I knew him, Ken never even changed his style of glasses. Like Bill, he preferred gold-wired aviators. Just because someone is wearing a certain type of frames in a photo doesn't mean that's the current style, it just might be what they like.

The first thing I did when I was trying to get clues from the color shot was to see if perhaps there were other pictures of Bill on the internet. I have an app that allows me to photograph a plant and have the software identify, within seconds, what species it is. I was hoping that perhaps he had appeared somewhere else online. I uploaded the books-and-sweater picture and asked to see similar images.

I guess I've seen too many movies. I don't know how sophisticated I thought the software would be, but I should have realized there wouldn't be a huge number of pictures of *any* specific octogenarian on the internet. I was rewarded with a screen full of middle-aged men in sweaters and glasses, none of whom looked like Bill. Well, what could I expect for free?

An interesting thing about the picture itself was that Bill was not looking at the photographer or camera. He was looking down at something, either on his lap or on a table.

We didn't know how my mother had come by the photo—whether she'd corresponded with him again or whether he'd initiated contact. Did he send her the picture or give it to her in person? Did she take the photo herself? How was it acquired? We didn't know *how* or *why* it came into her possession, but I feel we knew why she kept it, especially saving it with the other four pictures. Or…did he give her all five at the same time? Had she received the black-and-white images later in life?

I suggested to Esther that perhaps her grandma had been a stalker, surreptitiously taking a photo of Bill from outside a coffee shop or bookstore. The image of my mom going to that great length, all cloak-and-dagger, was hilarious. We got a good laugh out of it.

"But seriously," she said, "who sends a picture of themselves in profile? Maybe she asked someone to take it for her." I could not imagine Mom bringing a co-conspirator into the saga.

I thought more about the setting. I wished the photograph had been printed in higher resolution so I could see what the book titles were. She had mentioned that "an old boyfriend" was a teacher in Connecticut, so I assumed this was in a high school library or classroom, maybe taken by the yearbook editors. Yet it wasn't a typical yearbook photo; he wasn't smiling or looking straight at the camera.

Of course, the next mystery was how the photo got to her. Did he voluntarily send it and say, "Hi, Ellen, this is me, how are you?" Did she write to him first, ask him how he was, and give her own photo? Did they meet face-to-face? That was too much to even imagine. If he were on the sixty-plus end of the scale, that could have taken place after my father had passed away. Did my mother reach out at that time? Did Bill read my father's obituary in the *New York Times* and send a letter of condolence along with the photo? What would have been the intent of such a letter?

So many unanswered questions.

I again voiced my wishes for an intelligence agent or Kremlin-ologist. Esther agreed it would be great to have a specialist help us pinpoint his age. "Otherwise, we will always be wondering."

She had to get back to caring for baby Oriyah, but she thanked me for the distraction.

"I'm glad I brightened your evening. It's fun to think about this rather than to think about sad grandma. We'll talk again soon."

"I completely agree and I thank you. You gave me a very good feeling. I miss her more in a good way now Lol."

A few moments later, she wrote, "I just can't, it keeps hitting me!"

I replied, "Grandma had a life!"

"Unbelieeeeveabllle!"

Chapter 18
New Perspectives

The burst of enthusiasm from Esther stimulated yet more outreach.

During this terrible year of loss, there were very few relatives remaining from my parents' generation. I was grateful that group included Michael's Aunt Rita.

Along with being an adoring wife and raising six kids, Rita had a career as a nurse practitioner and therapist, specializing in eating disorders. She is an artist, hostess, and lover of music and travel. She is perpetually the charmer, the life of the party. She manages to keep tabs on nieces and nephews; first, second, and even third cousins; visiting Israeli students who came to her home; old friends from her youth in the Albany/Great Barrington area… and everywhere she goes, she makes new connections, too. Rita is a treasure.

One thing that would come as no surprise to anyone is that Rita had been extremely popular in her youth. Her future husband had to wait weeks to have dates with her because her calendar was so full. He was persistent, however, and ultimately won her over. She never regretted her choice.

She lost her husband in the summer of 2022, and we lost his brother, Ken, less than six months later. It had been a rough time for the family, and I was grateful for every visit we had with her.

Rita was doing a sort of road tour, staying for a week or two with each of her children while waiting for her home to sell. I never quite knew where she would be, but thanks to cell phones, I could always find her if I wanted to chat.

She called me a few days after my text exchange with Esther. "So, what's new?" she asked.

I told her I had quite a story if she had time to listen. I gave her the rundown: from finding the photos to calling Mom's friend; looking through her address book, the commencement list, yearbooks; and contacting the churches. "I think we've reached a dead end," I said, "but that doesn't mean it's not a story worth telling."

"Oh, don't give up! There's got to be another way. Maybe he was in a fraternity or something? If you can figure out what fraternity he was in, you can contact their national office."

That didn't seem likely. If I couldn't find his name, how would I know whether he'd been in a fraternity? I told her I'd send the photos and we should talk again soon.

That started a barrage of texts, back and forth. If I'd been looking for a Kremlinologist, Aunt Rita was it! She said, "He doesn't have a lot of money. He's not wearing a suit, but rather a sports coat and pants that don't match. But they're at a party…"

She was trying to figure out from the decorations in the room what holiday it might be or if it was, as she suspected, a fraternity event. She had all sorts of theories.

"One thing's for sure," I joked, after she talked about his lack of funds, "they couldn't afford many chairs."

"I'm not going to give up on this, I'm going to keep brainstorming. You should too, Karen."

Her clear fascination with the puzzle and conviction that we were going to find out more boosted my spirits. There might be other sources of information.

A thought occurred to me. Mom had alluded to Bill, although not by name, twice in the almost sixty years that I knew her. In the four years when I was away at college, my younger sister still lived with our parents. Who knows how many conversations she might have had with Mom during that time? Perhaps during one of the hundreds, Mom had referenced Bill. I didn't want any resistance from my siblings on this project, but I'd be an idiot to pass up interviewing a primary source if my sister had stories to share.

That afternoon, around dinner time, I sent her a text.

"Are you still working? Can you talk?"

"What's up?" she asked.

"Complicated," I texted. "Call when you can."

She had a few loose ends on reports to complete before she was able to call. Finally, the phone rang.

"So, what is it?"

"I'm working on something, and I don't want you to push back with questions and tell me not to do it or anything, but I was wondering… Do you remember Mom ever saying anything about old boyfriends?"

She paused to think it over. I'm sure this wasn't a subject she had expected to discuss.

"Well, there was that guy she was pinned to when she met Dad, and I know she broke that off really quickly. She never talked about anybody else that I can remember, but I'm sure she dated."

I agreed. We talked for a few minutes about her kids, the status of the house sale and all the other estate headaches, and then I let her go. While our conversation hadn't broken any new ground for me, it did confirm that Mom wasn't the type to go blabbing about her past, and clearly there was no other man she talked about except Dad. Those two times she said something to me—really, a total of maybe three sentences—were *it*…the only time she'd ever spoken about Bill to anyone other than Dad or Sally.

I reconsidered the concept of creating my own interpretations, using fiction to fill in what might have happened. There was also that lingering mystery about the fifth photo and how Mom came to have it. If I was going to guess about Bill's history, his name, and his identity, surely I must be allowed to create a story about how she got another picture of him.

Chapter 19
Back to Basics

The conversation with my sister left me pretty disappointed. Yet another dead end. I was pouting to myself. I didn't *want* to have to do creative writing, I wanted facts. I knew there was more to the story. There had to be a concrete truth somewhere out there.

Aunt Rita had been confident we'd be able to find more detail. Her conviction sparked me to do something I hadn't done in over a month: go back and look at the yearbooks again.

While we didn't know his last name, we had a vague idea of where he came from, and we had several photos. It occurred to me that I should stop looking at the names and focus, instead, on the faces. Maybe he really did graduate in one of those classes and we just had the wrong name.

I began with the composite photos of fraternity brothers, but the individual headshots were so tiny, you really couldn't tell one person from another. Fortunately, there were all kinds of clubs depicted, not just fraternities. I started to review the yearbook, page by page, scrutinizing photos rather than names.

Around page 48, in the "Future Teachers' Club," I spotted a guy who resembled the young man in Mom's photos. It certainly looked more like him than any of the Williams had—there was that fair hair and straight nose again. The names of the club members were listed under the photo, and his appeared as "P. Dartley."

I immediately turned to the senior section. There was Philip Dartley, smiling that same gentle smile as "Bill," with a hometown designation of Brookfield, Connecticut.

I took photos of the club picture and Philip Dartley's senior portrait and texted them to Sally for confirmation.

"What do you think?" I asked.

She replied within seconds. "Yes, yes, yes that is indeed him… your mom's Phil."

All this time she'd been saying it was "Bill," and I'd been looking for anybody with the first name—or even possibly middle name—of William. She was confident, even emphatic, in her response: "Oh yes, of course that's Phil, that's him." Talk about a red herring!! I had to forgive her, it had been seventy years or more since she'd even thought about him—and at least the names rhymed. It was frustrating, though, since so much of my earlier detective work had hinged on getting his first name right.

I thanked her for the corroboration and started reaching out to my enthusiastic support team to let them know we'd found our man…or his name, anyway.

Elizabeth went back to the Penwell graduation roll for 1956 and found his full name: Philip Richard Dartley. Thus equipped, I went on to look for other possible online information: property records, employment records, marriage records… Even though he was born in the 1930s, it was reasonable to expect he had left a footprint on the internet.

Using his complete name, I came up with three different prop-erty listings and addresses. Two were in Connecticut, and one was in Florida. Not knowing which was correct—e.g., whether he'd relocated within Connecticut while keeping an address in Florida for snow-birding—I decided I would send the same letter to all three locations.

> *Dear Mr. Dartley:*
>
> *I have been looking for you because you were a friend of my mother, Ellen (née Kalt). I think you knew one another in the early 1950s, sometime around 1952 or 1953.*
>
> *Mom passed away recently, after a long decline during COVID isolation. Among her personal effects were some photos of you, and she had mentioned you in the past.*
>
> *I hope you don't find this too intrusive, but I was hoping that perhaps you could tell me a little bit more about my mom from those years. I'm providing my home address as well as email and phone numbers, if you'd like to get in touch.*
>
> *Thank you so much for your time.*

I prepared envelopes for each of the three addresses, but before affixing stamps, I decided to try one more thing. I typed in his name with the word "obituary." The first thing that came up was an obit-uary for his stepmother.

The next thing I found was a link to a YouTube video with his name as the title.

It was a lovely photo montage set to music. It looked like one of his grandchildren must have put it together, with photos starting from his babyhood through childhood, then young adulthood—in-cluding a photo that was contemporaneous with the ones with my mom, even wearing that same sports jacket and slacks. There was no mistaking his sweet smile.

The montage continued with images from a wedding; then young parenthood, Super Bowl parties, cub scout meetings, family vacations with minigolf and pedal-boating. There was a retirement party, scenes with grandchildren who gradually got older. And of course, as indicated from the first slide, the fact that he had passed away in 2017.

I was saddened to think that I missed connecting with him, yet I felt I had a real glimpse into who he was. The man in the slideshow seemed sweet and happy. He reminded me of my father-in-law, unpretentious and devoted to family. It looked like he'd had a good life. The list of names at the end of the video indicated stepchildren, and I realized that his widow was, in fact, his second wife.

Although I obviously couldn't send the letter to him, and I would not want to upset his biological children, I thought it might be all right to reach out to his second wife / widow. After all, there's no way she would have seen my mom as a threat. They must have met long after he knew my mother.

So, I switched up the letter a little bit, explaining the situation in more detail. I had found on that video that her name was Linda, and I wrote:

> *Dear Mrs. Dartley:*
> *Please accept my apology for intruding into your life, but I'm hoping that you can do me a tremendous favor.*
> *First, let me express my condolences for the loss of your late husband, Phil. I hope you have been comforted by your family and all your happy memories together.*
> *I recently experienced my own loss. My parents met in 1955 and had a wonderful marriage, but it was tragically cut short. My dad passed away from cancer in October, 2000. Mom survived him by 23 years and a day. Sadly, she had progressive dementia for the last four of those years, but I was able to help her*

remain in her home, as I lived only about 15 minutes away from her in New Jersey. I was with her when she passed, peacefully, three months ago.

While going through my mother's personal effects, my daughter found some photos of my mom, in her teens, with a young man who most definitely was not my father.

I knew immediately "who" it was, although I'd never known your husband's name. My mother had mentioned, once or possibly twice in all the 58 years that I knew her, that there had been one other very special person in her life before she met my dad. All I knew was that he wasn't Jewish (we are), and that he had eventually become a teacher in Connecticut.

I took many clues from the photos. The young man was wearing a Penwell College sweatshirt, and a second photo showed a foursome which included my mother's best chum, Sally. Fortunately, Sally is still alive, and she was able to give me a little bit more insight.

Bottom line: through much sleuthing, I was able to figure out that the charming young man who clearly made a significant impression on my mom was your husband, Phil. When I finally found his name, I was gratified to see what a beautiful life he'd led, through the memorial video that your granddaughter put together. He looked like a wonderful man.

I don't know if I'm asking too much to have you write, or even perhaps speak with me, so that I might get a little more insight. It's a huge imposition and I understand if you say "no," or ignore me completely, but on the other hand I'd be so grateful to get a fuller glimpse into my mother's youth.

Obviously, these things happened over 70 years ago, well before you met him, but it's possible that at some point in your many years together he might have mentioned my mother. To recap: her maiden name was Ellen Kalt and she lived in Manhattan. She and Sally would come up to visit Sally's grandparents who lived in Fairfield. I am assuming that they knew one another sometime in the period of 1952/1953.

I apologize for intruding into your peaceful life. If you are willing to contact me, please use the information below.

Thank you for your time, and again, I'm so sorry for your loss. He seemed like a very sweet man.

Chapter 20
More Insight

"**I** can't believe you reached out to his widow," said Elizabeth. "She's going to be so offended."

"I think my tone was appropriate. I didn't demand anything, I just explained who I was and said I'd be grateful for the chance to talk about him with her. It's been six years or more since he passed, she must be used to it by now. It's worth a shot. Who knows? He may have never mentioned Mom to her."

I explained to Elizabeth how I had figured that the widow was a much better bet, as a contact, than his kids, who might harbor resentment about their dad's old girlfriend. Since Mom predated Linda by such a long time, I found it less likely that she would be upset.

I told Esther what I'd done. She was still marveling at how quickly I'd tracked down such minutiae. She, too, was sad he had passed away.

"But man, you're like a boarhound. Once you get that scent, you don't let up," she said.

"I just use the tools available. I figured I'd follow the leads, and I was so glad there were some answers."

In hindsight, the whole thing came together pretty quickly. I was stagnant for almost two months, hitting dead ends with the yearbooks and the church—really, because I was hung up on the name Bill. But once my team of supporters boosted my energy and enthusiasm, I dove right back in and found answers.

Less than a week after I figured out Phil's name from the club photo, my cell phone rang. Caller ID showed the name as Linda Dartley.

The fact that she was calling at all was a good sign. She could have just flat out ignored me. I took a deep breath before I answered the phone.

"Hello?"

Linda identified herself.

I said, "Oh my goodness, thank you so much for responding. I wasn't sure how you would feel about being contacted."

She was kind and generous with her time. We spent about twenty-five minutes on the phone, and she allowed me to ask all sorts of questions. I told her about the purpose of my project, and that I was so grateful she was taking part. I explained that I hadn't wanted to reach out to his children or his first wife, and she understood. I offered to change some of the identifiable details about him for my book so it wouldn't upset his family, and she felt that would be a good idea.

Had she known that Phil once dated a New York City girl? Oh, yes, he'd spoken about Ellen several times. For a country boy like him, it was a big deal to go down to New York. He'd even managed to hitchhike there for one of his visits.

Was his father really a minister? No, that was his grandfather. But his parents were dead set against him being with a Jewish girl. His mother told him it would kill his father. His father told him that his mother would kill herself.

This was completely consistent with my take on the situation. I'd always suspected the resistance was from Phil's family rather than my mother's, especially since Estelle had such minimal identification with being Jewish. It was common for nineteenth-century German Jewish Americans to assimilate; she had become as German as she could.

I asked Linda when she and Phil had gotten married, and she explained that his first marriage did not go well. He tried to make it work for years, but they officially split in the early 1980s. She and Phil got married in 1984 and spent thirty-three years together.

From the video's mention of stepchildren, I surmised that she'd also had a previous marriage. She explained that she, too, had been divorced and that was how she and Phil had met—in a divorced parents' support group. "We were friends long before we started dating."

I saw their relationship timeline as the perfect opening to get that final piece of information. "I know it's awkward, but my daughter and I have this big mystery around the fact that there was a fifth photo, a color photo taken some time later than the original ones. We can't figure out if or how they were in touch again."

"Oh, yes," said Linda. "That was before my time. He and Ellen met up to talk…once. It was before his marriage ended." She was unperturbed. It seemed like my mother had sought him out, not for anything romantic, but simply for some kind of closure.

Linda shared a few more stories about Phil's life. He had indeed been a high school teacher. He returned to his hometown area after Penwell. He loved camping and being with family. Toward the end of his life he, too, had dementia. "Phil was wonderful, just the kindest man," she said.

Linda shared another fact. "One of the reasons Phil told me stories about Ellen was because I'm Jewish, too."

This, reader…this is why I always felt it was important to find the actual story. I have never seen a better example of truth being stranger than fiction; I could not have anticipated such a twist, and frankly, I would never have made it up because it would seem so implausible.

This sparked even more questions for Linda. I tried not to bombard her, but I obviously wanted to know everything about how they managed to be together. I asked her if her first husband was Jewish and what her previous experience had been with interfaith relationships.

"Well, when I was younger, I was engaged to a non-Jewish man and my parents did the same kind of thing as Phil's. They threatened to sit shiva, cut me out of their lives as if I were dead. They would not give their consent for me to marry that boy, so we broke it off. A year or two later, I married someone Jewish. We raised two kids, but like I said, I had to leave him. He was a terrible person."

Linda said she and Phil were aware that they'd been given a second chance to marry for love, regardless of religious differences. Especially with the older generation no longer having the same control over their choices, they both felt that they had "righted a wrong, that it was some kind of poetic justice."

Indeed.

Chapter 21

Digression—A Bird May Love a Fish

When Mom and Phil were dating, in the 1950s, the exogamy/intermarriage rate between Jews and gentiles was less than 5 percent.

According to a 1957 survey taken in the United States, compared to Catholics and Protestants, Jewish people were least likely to intermarry. There was certainly interfaith dating away from watchful eyes, "for practice," but when things got serious, and public, there were plenty of examples of parents on either side who threatened, "Over my dead body." It was a common reason for an engagement—and a heart—to be broken. We know that Linda and Phil's parents each had such reactions.

Interfaith marriage rates for Jews rose over time as the generations became more assimilated. Jeff's family was already more established in America, and Estelle did everything she could to erase her Eastern European Jewish roots. I don't believe she would have raised a fuss about Mom "marrying out."

In many cases, second- and third-generation American Jews loosened their hold on their religiosity. In the last decades of the twentieth century, American culture as a whole became more inclusive, and Jews stood out less. Some—but not all—previously exclusive clubs, colleges, and corporations became more integrated as time went on.

In the thirty years or so between when Mom knew Phil and when he married Linda, things had changed considerably. It was obvious that their aging parents should have no say in the matter, but it wasn't just about parental approval. According to a study by the Pew Foundation, Jews in second marriages after divorce had a much higher exogamy rate than those marrying for the first time.

Jewish American culture had evolved. Rates of intermarriage rose among non-Orthodox Jews to the point where, of the marriages that have taken place since 2000, it was found that 28 percent non-Orthodox Jews had married other Jews, while 72 percent had married someone who had not previously identified as Jewish. Some spouses converted to Judaism; other couples raised their children with two religions, or none at all.

So much for statistics. Anecdotally, I wanted to know something about those rare couples who intermarried in the 1950s: Could I find an example? How had their marriage happened? Had it been successful?

I spoke with a friend whose mother was Jewish and father was Italian Catholic, both from Brooklyn. Her parents' story had its own twists and turns. It is only quite recently that she found out a family secret: her mother had been previously married, in her late teens, to a Jewish boy—but it was a disastrous match and they got a quick divorce.

She had an active social life in the years that followed, eventually having a long-term relationship with an Italian Catholic man seven years her senior. When she hit her early thirties, she announced it was time for them to get married, since she wanted to have children. Neither family raised an objection.

This bears out much of what the studies indicated. Even during a time of low intermarriage like the 1950s, either a divorced person or an "older" person was more likely to marry outside their faith.

In the case of my friend's parents, the groom was already in his late thirties. He had been sent to a Protestant private school as a teenager, and had never been an observant Catholic; coincidentally, his brother also married a Jewish girl and had a solid marriage. No one on his side had a problem with his marrying his Jewish girlfriend. The bride's mother, a widow, was happy to see her daughter settle down, as long as her grandchildren were raised Jewish. They were.

Chapter 22

Report to the Club

The evening after my phone call with Linda, I was on a three-way text of the "Ellen Fan Club" with Esther and Elizabeth when I shared the salient tidbit about Linda's past. Elizabeth's mind was blown.

"She's Jewish?"

"Yup."

Esther, on the other hand, was confused. "Wait, you mean he was Christian?"

I must have left the interfaith dating out of the story when I told her. It had been shocking enough that her grandmother was with someone other than her grandfather; I didn't even bring up the fact he wasn't of the same faith. She absorbed the information without further hesitation.

"What an amazing story," she said. "It sounds like he was a nice man."

"Yes," I wrote, "and I thought it was good that Mom eventually got closure."

Sally hadn't really given me insight as to whether things had ended quickly or were drawn out, but I imagine that Mom's heartache must have lasted a while. She was alone, at least not serious with anybody, for a couple of years before she met my father. That's what Dad meant when he told me, "Now you're ready."

"How do you think she found Phil again? Where would they have met?" Esther asked. "I mean, this was way before the internet."

I had given this some thought. Up until 1981, my family lived in Maryland, and my mother wouldn't have been able to just dash off to New England for an afternoon.

Except… My brother started as a freshman at Yale in 1978, and Jojo joined him up in New Haven in 1980. At some point, Mom surely had access to a Connecticut phone book. Perhaps she looked up Phil's information and asked if they could meet for coffee. The timeline matched: it was toward the end of the bad marriage but before the divorce and his marrying Linda.

I never thought that the meeting or the photo took place after my father died. Phil didn't look like he was sixty-five in the photo, and there's no way that in her grief, living in New Jersey, Mom would have bothered to go up to Connecticut. Nope, clearly their reunion took place during my siblings' college era.

So that part of the mystery was solved—or at least I had drafted a highly plausible scenario. I was really proud of Mom for taking that extra step, reconnecting with him to learn who and what he had become.

"It's funny," I said to Esther. "There are many paths to happiness." Mom might have been happy with Phil, except that his parents were so against the relationship. But she was truly happy with my dad. They were a great match and they supported one another through both hard and good times. They raised four children, went through financial challenges and success, career highs and lows, and the loss of three of their four parents (since Sarah outlived my dad).

Mom was never the same without Dad. She had friends and kept active. She traveled, she saw her grandchildren, but really my father was her best friend, companion, and the love of her life.

This whole episode involved a long-distance romance, something one might even call "forbidden fruit" since Phil wasn't Jewish. Sally said they felt like big shots having college boyfriends, but I can see from the pictures that Mom simply enjoyed being with him. And that look on her face? This was a girl who knew how to live.

I feel incredibly fortunate to have had the opportunity to encounter this version of my mom—this rebellious, independent, happy, adventurous, sneaky young woman who was able to do what she wanted without her ever-disapproving mother's supervision. It was sometime after that innocent time of bike riding in hallways, and before the days of being a college student and then a young wife and mother. It was an aspect of her personality, and her life, that I'd never known before, and it was a privilege—for both me and Elizabeth—to discover her.

Afterword

When my father was in the hospital, my mother held a constant vigil at his bedside. She sent me to pick out adjacent cemetery plots and make other funeral preparations; we knew his demise was imminent.

While Dad dozed in and out of consciousness, Mom reviewed cards and printed emails that friends had sent, saving them to read aloud when he was awake. She screened his phone calls and restricted his visitors. Most importantly, Mom—not a writer, per se—spent hours crafting an epic, paid obituary for the *New York Times*, making certain his legacy would be acknowledged. There was also a formal article by a *Times* staffer, as well as a paid tribute from some of his research colleagues; later articles appeared in other newspapers and professional publications.

After my father-in-law's passing, Sue made sure to submit a full obituary to the *Star-Ledger*. Except for his college and graduate school days and their early married years in the Boston area, Ken had spent his entire life in New Jersey, and this was the paper that meant the most to him.

I mentioned earlier that among Mom's archives were dozens of obituaries of old friends. By the time she passed, there weren't many contemporaries of hers left to contact. She had ten grandchildren and fifteen great-grandchildren—quite a legacy—but I never actually submitted anything to a newspaper.

My son made sure there would be an article in the Barnard alumni publication, but remarked that he was disappointed, if not outright upset, that I hadn't made more of an effort to publicly memorialize his grandmother.

Michael pointed out, "Your mom has written an entire book about her."

Acknowledgements

First props go to the incredibly detail-oriented "snooping around" by Elizabeth. I never could have gotten the puzzle box open—-but I still get credit for knowing the exact significance of what she found.

Thank you to those who helped me through the difficult years of Mom's decline, especially Johni, Benta, and Mercy.

Thank you to those friends and family who have supported me on the project: Terry, Sandy, Esther, Rita, Jaci, Christina, Barbara, Eileen, Nicole, Nina, Carlyn, Alice... Man, I really can't keep a secret, can I?

Finally, thank you, Mom, for passing along your rebellious spirit. Thanks for keeping the photos, too—I believe you meant them to be found, and I am forever grateful for getting the opportunity to "meet" this part of you.

About the Author

Karen Gooen has been a writer—primarily of non-fiction—for over forty years, focusing on sports, medicine, and travel. Only in the past decade did she tackle the topic of American Mah Jongg, first with her memoir/manual, *Searching for Bubbe Fischer*, and then two novels in the Mah Jongg Table Talk Tale series.

This is her fourth book.